KIND OF PERSON

Finding Meaning in Customer Service

NICOLE BLOCK, MBA

PASSIONPRENEUR®
PUBLISHING

Publishing information
Publishing and design facilitated by Passionpreneur Publishing
A division of Passionpreneur Organization Pty Ltd
ABN: 48640637529

Melbourne, VIC | Australia
www.passionpreneurpublishing.com

To my husband, Corrie, who walked into my life like a lightning bolt, striking the earth and shaking the road I walked on. He has believed in me like no other and supported me even in my craziest ideas. You are my favorite person and best friend. I Dcuk you!

FOREWORD

BY MAYA MATTAR, #1 BESTSELLING AUTHOR, FOUNDER & DIRECTOR OF LASTING IMPRESSIONS.

Nicole Block has written a manifesto on the meaning of work across all customer service industries. I personally resonate with customer service as a calling, rather than just a job. I knew from a very young age that my function in this world would always be in service provision to others. I enjoy improving the quality of people's lives through the products and services I have represented over the years, and like Nicole, I find tremendous meaning now in serving others by leading them to do the same.

Can I confess to something?

Ok, I assume you said yes. Here we go! I did not specifically choose a career in customer service. I chose a career that would help me discover the world, a career that would nurture my curiosity, a career that would allow me to meet people and, most importantly, would satisfy my thirst to learn and grow. I chose to be part of a cabin crew for an airline, a childhood dream that came true in 2003. A dream that evolved and here I am, two decades later, with a fulfilling career in the service industry.

My career in customer service took me around the globe, and made me my own boss and an Amazon bestselling author. I do not pretend to know it all, but I know that to reach a state of service excellence we need to serve ourselves consistently with the necessary dose of knowledge, skills, and attitude, lots of reflection, and continuously evolve and upgrade our standards. We can't serve others well if we do not serve ourselves first.

Everyone can give and everyone can serve but very few people can be generous in their giving and in their serving. Generosity is one of the main differentiators in customer service, and this is what makes people excel in the service industry. My generosity and my passion to give and share got me into customer service and to where I am today.

They say that "good service begins at the top" but I would say it begins with *you*!

Customer service is not a department—it is an attitude and a mindset that should be integrated into the organizational culture and individual minds whenever they are in the business of serving others. And Nicole illustrates this in an elaborate manner in this beautiful book *Kind of Person*.

In an increasingly competitive, constantly changing world, creating the best possible experience for the customer has never been more important. Achieving excellence, when you can serve others and consistently leave them with a positive memorable experience – a lasting impression – is crucial to individual and business success.

I have stopped treating people the way I would like to be treated a long time ago, when I realized that I can do it better. Now I treat people the way they would like to be treated. For me, personally connecting on an emotional level with customers, providing them with efficient service and ensuring high quality, is my go-to formula that can help every person who is at the service of others to achieve excellence: Service Excellence = Emotional Connection x Efficiency x Quality.

I've always found that those who thrive in customer service do so because of certain qualities that allow them to add value in the process of serving. In this world, where everyone seems to have to have their say all the time, and the most important voice is our own, it's imperative for customer service agents to be equipped with what it takes to make them stand out.

Readers can expect to come away from this book with a profound sense of pride and purpose in their vocation in customer service. This is especially for those who may have been struggling with recognizing their chosen profession as a calling rather than a stepping stone to another career. Customer service is a career. It is how people are helped, served, and cared for, and deserves to be recognized independently as a powerful act of community creation.

You will also benefit from the tips and tricks in leadership that will help you to develop your own customer service teams or organization as a leader. You will learn how to quickly form a high-functioning team, and how to help your teammates work well together by choosing the right mindset. And you will also benefit from the very practical tools aimed to help you and your team turn a negative customer experience into a positive one, using the often-limited resources available to you.

Kind of Person is a meaningful and practical celebration of the profession of customer service, and a must-read for any leader of a customer-facing team.

CONTENTS

ACKNOWLEDGEMENTS

I would like to acknowledge my right hand, Diona, for never doubting my ideas and thought processes. You were 100% onboard from the start and put 150% in at all times, without any complaints. The results we have seen would not have been possible without your leadership, dedication and delivery on the promises we made to the crew!

My mentor team: Ruaan, Alex, Marina, Bogdan, Claudia, and Balazs. You really stepped up to the challenge on this one. All the classroom training in the world won't change anything. It has been your persistent dedication, leadership, coaching and mentoring of the cabin crew that has made this flower bloom. The feedback from the crew on your approach, support, advice and mentoring has been as close to perfection as anyone can get. Thank you, you have made a difference in each and every person's life you have coached! #nothingistoomuchtrouble

To my immediate manager, Jilly, thank you for believing in me and the program. I know you were taking a chance, but it paid off. We have more engaged and motivated crew who have found meaning in what they do. They are going onboard every day actively looking for ways to create unforgettable moments and experiences for our customers and our customers are rewarding us with loyalty.

To the crew who have attended the program, thank you for spending your time with me, for listening to something you haven't heard before, and for embracing the change. Your honesty and openness during the days we have spent together have been a breath of fresh air. I am so proud of all of you and I love hearing all the amazing things you are doing on board to create memorable reasons for customers to choose our airline. #makeadifference

INTRODUCTION

I have three young children: an eight-year-old boy and five-year old boy-girls twins. When the twins were thirteen months old, I separated from my now ex-husband. I was married for nearly ten years and had a really happy marriage. But things came to an amicable end, and if you've been through a divorce, it makes you sit back and re-evaluate your life and how you got to where you are. I realized that I had been doing everything for my family and was really just plodding along in life. I had a good job at IntrepidAir, but my job was just a job, and I didn't really look beyond that. My ex-husband's job always came first, and I was the one taking care of the household.

I was a passive participant in my own life, and often felt unjustly stuck between a failed marriage and a lackluster job. I felt like my life was something that was happening to me, something I needed to adapt to, react to, or absorb – something that I rarely had control over. I found meaning in being the martyr in my own story, and inwardly consoled myself with the pity and honor that such a martyr might deserve.

But then I met someone who completely changed the way I looked at my life and my work. A random stranger helped me to remove my blinders of victimhood and self-slavery and see the possibilities available to me and my control over them. I saw that my life was what I had made of it and that although sometimes I didn't like the choices that were available to me, they were my choices all the same. My life was the result of every decision I had ever made. My passivity fell away, and I decided to design my life in a new way, the way I really wanted it.

So just as companies have vision statements and values, I decided to do write them for myself, so I would have something to work towards. Think about it, if you don't have a vision for your life or a goal to work towards, you are never really going to achieve what you want. My vision statement is:

> "To balance my life between being a loving mother and devoted wife and working to be a successful career woman. I want to have fun in my life, collect experiences, not let time pass by without noticing it, and have no regrets."

From this, I looked at the values that are important to me and I live by which are:

kindness, being dependable, understanding,
honest, balanced, approachable, organized, and
justice-oriented.

Justice orientation is an important value to me because I believe that by acting according to what's fair, I gain trust and demonstrate responsibility.

Having a vision and values meant that I had things to work towards. I had always wanted to get an MBA, but this had always been reserved for my ex-husband. In my previous marriage, if either of us was going to do their MBA, it would have been my husband. But the world looked different after my divorce and writing my vision statement. I took responsibility and made dramatic decisions to change the experience of my life.

I signed up for my MBA, was awarded a full scholarship, and finished it 21 months later, earning a distinction in every subject. And that empowering stranger I met ... well, I married him.

When I am now faced with something, I know I always have a choice. I might not like my choices, and sometimes my choice is not to do anything about something at all, but I now own that. I don't think to myself, "well that happened to me," or, "I have no control over that." And the reason I wrote this book is that I want you to also see that you have a purpose for being in your work, you have choices, and you can control how your life turns out. And if I can do that for you then I will be a very happy person. And trust me, you will be happier too.

Maybe that's you ... plodding along in the customer service industry, watching your life happen to you and reacting to it as though your major function in life is to adapt to, rather than create your experience at work.

- What if you could find meaning and purpose in customer service without changing your job?
- What if you could have a happier experience at work every day?
- What if you could find joy in caring for your customers and colleagues?
- What if you could see what you are doing each day as a meaningful set of experiences that are mapping out a path for a fun and satisfying career?

Would you want that?

That's what I'm offering in this book. I'm offering a new paradigm for you to see what you do in the light of meaningful service, not only for your customers and organization but for you, personally. When customer service becomes something that you enjoy and take pride in, you will not only get more opportunities for promotions and salary increases, but you'll also have a more meaningful experience in the half of your life that you are spending at work.

I got my start in customer service long before I was born. I'm the product of a long line of ancestors that survived by adding value to their communities by being helpful. My dad has been in customer service in the automotive industry for more than five decades.

As a young girl of eight years, I would often accompany my father to work during my school vacations. He worked in the service area of an auto dealership and took care of customers needing their vehicles maintained or repaired. As the customers got their cars returned to them, they would be required to pay their invoices, and there was a cashier lady who collected payment at a separate window. This was in the days before computers, so everything was done on paper, with calculators, and 3-ply carbon paper invoices.

I used to hang out with the cashier lady, and she would give me a pencil and a stack of receipt paper, and I would click away on a little calculator next to me as customers came and went. I greeted them and pretended to collect their money as they paid the cashier lady. I would write unintelligible 3-ply receipts for them, ask them how their car service experience was that day, and thank them for their business.

Then I realized that the cashier lady herself could be my customer. I asked her if there was anything I could do to help her. She showed me a stack of unsorted invoices and receipt copies that needed to be filed. So, I sorted and filed them. Apparently,

I was pretty good at it, and since no one else wanted to do it, I got the job. My dad paid me a couple of bucks each time. It turned out that it had been a very long time since anyone wanted to do the file sorting, and there was a backlog of boxes with unsorted papers. My dad started to bring them home for me, and I would spend the weekend sorting them out so he could take them back to work fully organized the next week.

And that was it. I was in customer service.

I've been in customer service for more than 35 years now. I started working as a checkout operator in a supermarket. I've sold mobile phones, been a bartender, and worked in a video store (do you remember VHS?). I was a hostess, a receptionist, and then spent more than a decade in the air as cabin crew. After shifting to training and crew management, I realized that the affinity and passion I have for customer service didn't fade when I moved out of the plane and onto the ground. My crew are my customers now. I have thousands of them, and I want to make their experience at work as meaningful of an experience as possible. I serve my crew, and they serve our customers.

I provide services like on-time payment of their salaries in exchange for their efforts. I provide ongoing coaching and training for them in their jobs. I provide clarity in roles and responsibilities, so they can coordinate with each other on the team, and know who is responsible for what. I allocate the shared resources of our team to achieve maximum effectiveness. And I provide encouragement, support, and leadership to bring them together and keep them focused on our shared goals.

My crew *are* my customers.

That's an important thing to know because customers tend to lie to you. Approximately 91% of customers that have a complaint won't tell their service provider, but they will tell an average of fifteen other people. And one-third of customers say that they would consider switching service providers after just one instance of bad customer service.[1] This means for every customer service complaint you actually hear, there are 150 people out there who have heard some kind of complaint about your service. Well … it's not different when you are providing services to your employees so that they can provide services to your customers.

It's important to note that 91% of my staff who have a complaint about me, my team, or our company, won't tell us about it, but they will tell fifteen other people. This is a terrible truth that companies need to wrestle with. We must treat our employees as customers because whether we like it or not, they'll behave like customers. We need to be providing good services, at least enough to meet expectations, if we are to have good customer service providers for our customers.

---

1   Nextiva. 2021. 100 Essential Customer Service Statistics and Trends for 2021. Retrieved from https://www.nextiva.com/blog/customer-service-statistics.html

Perhaps you are a manager in the service of those in front-line customer service. Or perhaps you are in front-line service. In either instance, this book is for you. And by the end of this book, you will have a new understanding of your job, the impact you have each day on the lives of those in your care, and how to curate the experience of service for yourself, your customers, and your colleagues.

However, this book is not a quick-fix self-help book. You'll get real tips and tricks from me that you can put into practice. I'll give you step-by-step instructions for handling difficult service situations. And I'll provide examples for you to follow and emulate that will raise your level of service to those around you, not at your expense, but your pleasure.

By the end of this book, you will be able to:

1. Understand why you are here and not somewhere else
2. Apply tactics that motivate and engage your team
3. Achieve a working environment that encourages your team to excel
4. Identify ways to promote team effectiveness
5. Evaluate options during the decision-making process
6. Clarify what leadership really means
7. Create a coaching culture (instead of a telling culture)
8. Promote trust
9. Curate empowerment

Imagine yourself at the end of this book, empowered with a new paradigm, a new sense of purpose, and a new set of skills you can use to advance in your career.

I'll also be giving you brief writing exercises along the way, so you can apply the learning directly to your current role. So, you might want to have a notepad and a pen with you while you read this book.

Although what you are about to read applies to any customer service role, I am writing from the perspective of the airline industry, perhaps one of the most physically and emotionally taxing customer service jobs in the world. I don't want to use the name of any company officially, so in my stories I'll refer to a hypothetical airline named IntrepidAir.

I'm so excited that you've decided to join me on this journey. Thousands of my crew have already benefitted from what's to follow, and I know you will too. But in order for you to appreciate the incredible effort that has gone into this, and the amazing benefits that you will gain as a result, I'll need to introduce you to my airline.

1

WHAT KIND OF PERSON
ARE YOU?

In 2012, we started the Leadership Development program at IntrepidAir. At that time, we had aggressive plans for expansion. The economy was thriving, and a lot of companies were in growth mode, which meant that people needed to travel. The whole company was like a dry sponge suddenly chucked into a sea of opportunity. We couldn't recruit fast enough or buy enough planes. Rosters were busy and promotions were quick. It was a gold rush in aviation, and we were the brave prospectors mining the gap between the luxury airlines and the ultra-low-cost carriers.

In aviation, our profit is tied directly to the price of oil, which governs the majority of our operating expenses and determines our profit margins. Low oil prices in the early 2010s allowed us to fly more cheaply, lowering prices for customers, increasing demand, and requiring us to hire a new army of cabin crew. But the golden years never last. Oil prices were on a steady rise in 2017, peaking in 2018. That meant it cost us much more to fly, and with the competition fierce, our ability to raise prices was restricted, inevitably reducing our profits.

A rise in interest rates accompanied the rise in oil prices, further increasing costs. There were also unfavorable currency movements at that time. These economic issues were happening around all of us at the same time, without our permission, outside of our control. It was a kind of perfect storm, and, as any company would, we had to look at costs and how to reduce them. All departments were asked to look at cost reduction strategies. Recruitment and promotions company-wide were put on hold indefinitely. The gold rush was over.

Then in March 2019, as if to invite us as a company into some cosmic test of resilience, we saw the grounding of a quarter of our fleet for technical reasons. It was a gut punch. We were reeling from the hit, injured, gasping for air in the market, and struggling to balance under the complexity of challenges we faced. Then the unthinkable happened.

Less than a year later, the COVID-19 worldwide pandemic hit. Airlines around the world crumbled as our industry's largest-scale economic assault pounded away at us, month after crushing month. We watched our competitors fall on the battlefield of lockdowns, travel restrictions, and a new layer of global fear. A microscopic enemy declared war on the human race, and the airline industry bore the first and heaviest attack. Air Italy, Trans States Airlines, Compass Airline, CityJet, German Airlines, LATAM Airlines, One Airlines, Jet Time, and Interjet (among many others), folded under the weight of an imperceptibly tiny bug. Some fortunate competitors like Thai Airways and South African Airways survived because they were rescued from the fight by their stakeholder governments and dragged to economic safety by massive bailouts.

Millions of people around the world were without jobs and the way we lived and traveled changed in ways we never thought possible. We didn't know what was happening, how dangerous it was, or how we as a company were to survive it.

I remember my husband and me being in lockdown in Dubai. We didn't leave our house for 72 days straight. With my company in chaos mode, I worked around the clock to calm the fears of our staff, answer questions, manage COVID-positive crew members, create new policies and procedures, pivot our operations to flying cargo, and ease the fears of two thousand IntrepidAir colleagues watching airlines around the world cut jobs and shut down.

In the spring of 2021, a year into the pandemic, my seven-year-old son asked me, "Mommy, when will I be able to go out without wearing a mask again? Is it soon?" And it broke my heart because even by that time, we didn't know, and India was just entering its most dangerous spike in COVID-19 cases and deaths, and at IntrepidAir, we had to cut off service to one of our largest international markets yet again.

In the most understated terms, 2018–2021 was a very challenging time at IntrepidAir, but we survived. When everything in the world was uncertain and the ground beneath us was shaking, we leaned on the strongest asset we had: each other.

Who were we at IntrepidAir? Were we more company or community? How would we manage this airline apocalypse?

Our Intrepid CEO refused to let go of our community values. We valued each other over everything, and we had invested heavily in each other. He believed that if we were to survive this challenge, the only acceptable way was together. No forced redundancies. Zero. We offered redundancy to those that wanted it, and a few opted for that, but the vast majority were put on unpaid leave, which meant that they could keep their visas, healthcare, and staff travel benefits so that they could ride out the storm without losing their place in our community.

We offered the remainder of our staff voluntary leave. They had their visas, healthcare, and accommodation paid for, even though nearly every plane in our fleet was grounded. Those who remained working, including myself, were all on 50% pay, and my team and I were working around the clock to manage the battle. We survived because we fought for it, we worked together, and we carried each other.

At the turn of the 21st century, airlines were innovating annually. Lots of different competitive advantages were invented each year. Iterative improvements in the seating, the food, and the inflight entertainment were all changing the customer experience across the industry. But by 2015, this rapid succession of improvements was considered basic services. In an age of free inflight Wi-Fi and first-class shower spas, how does a low-cost carrier like IntrepidAir stand out? When seating, food, and entertainment have all been optimized, what differentiator is left that will be meaningful to a customer who experiences yesterday's delight as today's minimum expectation? It's us. It's our people. It's who we are as an economic tribe. We're the only truly meaningful differentiating variable left in the industry. That's how we survived. We had the right kind of people.

The gold we mined in the rush between 2010 and 2017 was the staff and crew we invited to join our community. And so, it should not have surprised us as much as it did that when the impacts from 2018 to 2021 came to test our strength, it was this hoard of gold we guarded most vigilantly.

It was our staff who had the power to make or break an IntrepidAir experience for our customers. And it was our leadership that could do the same for our staff.

We respected and trusted our staff. At that moment, 35,000 feet above the ground, there was no one onboard guiding them, looking over their shoulders. We knew that 90% of the outcomes of each flight would turn out was down to them – the crew. They were tasked to set the tone for the flight, create the right atmosphere, lead their team effectively, deliver an amazing customer experience, and curate the way their customers would feel. Miles above the earth, detached from management, all these things were in their hands.

> "People will forget what you said, people will forget what you did, but people will never forget how you made them feel."
>
> – Maya Angelou

You too, as a customer service agent, have the opportunity each day – interacting with the lives of your customers – to determine the quality of their experience with you and your corporate community. So, what kind of person do you want to be? What kind of agent of service do you want to be?

Many people will never discover or embrace the kind of person they really are at work because they're too busy pretending to be something they're not: a victim, a slave, or an idiot.

We've all heard the complaints of those colleagues and co-workers who talk about their work as though it's a series of uncontrollable events happening to them, rather than a set of experiences they are participating in. They talk about how they are being treated by the company, how much they wish their boss didn't suck so much, or how they feel bullied by others they work with. In reality, these employees are empowered actors in their lives. No one forced them into their job. They're not victims. They're just pretending.

No one was standing over them with a gun when they were presented with an employment contract, and they accepted the deal that was offered to them. They were made an offer, and they accepted the deal freely and fairly. They made an agreement with a community to provide a service, which they are now unlikely to be providing at the level they agreed to. And yet, they feel justified in the hypocrisy of complaining about the services of their company. It's ridiculous. They are pretending to be victims when, in fact, they're 100% complicit in their own unhappiness.

And no one is making them stay in their current jobs either. They are free to leave at any time. They can simply walk away if they're unhappy. We live in an age when most people will be cared for, protected, fed, and clothed, even if they are not working for pay. Most people have friends, family, or at least live in a society that will help them stay above the poverty line. It may not be comfortable to walk away from your work, but if you're truly unhappy, how much better is it to at least try to be happy somewhere else? Yet so many are content to pretend that they are slaves, when in fact they are 100% empowered to leave at any time they want.

And still, others pretend to be idiots. Only an idiot would out-source the direction of their life to an employer. Are they really going to give someone else that power? Not likely. In fact, every decision they've ever made in their entire lives led them to that particular job at that particular time. It's not an accident that they're there. At the time they entered their economic community, they believed that that particular job was their fastest road to success. Because if there was a better way, they'd be doing that instead. But they're not doing something else instead. Why? Because they're not idiots. They're just pretending to be.

And what a sad waste of energy is it for any person to spend half of their lives pretending to be a victim when they are empowered, a slave when they are free, or an idiot when they are pursuing their best path to success? It's a tragic waste of half of a life.

I say half of a life because that's what work is. It's half of your life. You spend roughly a third of your life sleeping. Of the time you spend conscious and awake, half of it will be at work. Your life is made up of a long series of experiences, more than half of which will likely be gained at work. And if work makes up half (or more) of your life, wouldn't you want it to be a meaningful half?

One of the best things I've done at IntrepidAir was to remind our staff that for as long as they are working with us, IntrepidAir is half of their conscious human experience. So, if you are in IntrepidAir for twelve years, like I have been, then six years of your conscious experience has been here at work, at IntrepidAir. You can't distance yourself from that. So, the idea that it is just a job really isn't true. It's half of your life. And whatever time you invest in that half of your life, you will never get it back. Half of you is the job you're in. If you are going to spend half of your life at IntrepidAir, we want it to be a good half. We want you to enjoy it, we want you to have fun and we want to make sure it gives life to you. This should be true for you too.

But what if you are not enjoying the experience of the half of your life that you are spending at work? You have two choices:

1. You can change where you spend half of your life; or
2. You can change the experience of the half of it that you do spend there

In other words, you can change your job, or you can change your mind. You're not stuck. You're not a victim or a slave, and only an idiot would want to not enjoy half of their life. The great thing is you can change your experience of a job you are already in.

So, let's say you want to start living a more meaningful life, and you'd like to start by changing your experience of your job rather than changing your job itself. Here's how you can start: connect with the people around you.

Did you know that the majority of the variance in whether or not an employee finds their job meaningful is in their relationships with the people around them at work? They don't need to connect with everyone in the company. They just need to connect with the three to five people they work with most often. And the most important of those relationships is with their line manager. The Gallup study found that 70% of the variance on employee engagement comes down to the relationship of the employee with their manager[2]. That means 70% of your team's engagement will be determined by their manager. Are you the manager?

So, make a note of the three to five people that you work with most, and don't leave out your line manager.

1. _____

2. _____

3. _____

---

2   Clifton, J., J. Harter. (2019) It's the Manager. Gallup Press, USA.

4. _____

5. _____

Ok, so you have your three to five people, but how do you connect with them?

Well, you can't do it just by looking from the outside.

If you look at a satellite image on Google Maps of an area – what does it tell you?

You can see roads, you can see there are lakes, seas, and distance between places. Not everyone will interpret the map in the same way, some will find more detail than others, and some highlight different things. But all will agree that from an aerial view, it's difficult to get an accurate picture of what the area actually looks like.

But what if you double-click and head down to the street view? What do you see then? You won't just see streets and roofs. You might see cars, people, tall buildings, trees. It's a totally different view, but of the exact same place. When you drill down a bit, you can see what was unseen in the 40,000-foot view.

The same principle applies when you interact with other people. If you just look at the surface, like the satellite image, you will miss all the unseen parts.

So how do you double-click on a person? Conversation.

Building relationships and taking the time to emotionally connect with people and get to know them is how we move from the satellite view to the street view on people. And it's those previously 'unseen' parts of us that ultimately impact the way we behave and build relationships at work. And those relationships ultimately determine our experience of work itself. Remember, you don't care nearly as much about what you're doing as you do about who you're doing it with.

If you were to take the time to really understand what lies beneath the surface for some of your colleagues what would it be like? What would be the benefit?

1. You might stop reacting to things they say or do.
2. You might understand why they are acting in a certain way.
3. You might be able to understand their point of view.
4. You might take the time to understand them better.
5. You will be more aware of what's important to them.

And don't forget, you might also make more money and live longer. Those are also known side effects of living a more meaningful and connected life.

To know what is important to another person and to understand their values and beliefs allows us to step into their shoes.

Connecting with someone on this level helps us to feel strong, supported, and confident.

When it is professionally appropriate, be personal with the people you work with. Talk to the people you work with, get to know them. Tell stories. Obviously, in the service industry, you need to be mindful to ensure that you don't talk about inappropriate things within earshot of your customers. I constantly remind my crew that their passengers are always within hearing distance. There are no invisible doors between the galley and the cabin.

Humans build trust through transparency. Offering information about yourself and asking them about themselves will help you and your colleagues and customers to enjoy each other's company. It doesn't need to be very deep and personal stuff, it could be as simple as showing an interest in where their next vacation will be, or whether or not they've tried the new restaurant in town. Remember, enjoying the company of the people you are working with is the same as enjoying your job.

Can you think of a time when it should've been the worst day at work ever, but because of the team at work, it turned out to be one of your best? What was it about the team at work that day that turned the experience around? If you enjoy the company of the people you are with, then it won't matter what work you are doing.

I remember when I was cabin crew at my previous airline. We were doing a long-haul fourteen-hour flight. About five hours into the flight half of the crew were on rest, sleeping in the hidden bunks under the floor, and I was left in charge. Two of my crew were newbies in their first month of flying. One of them ran to me to tell me that a passenger had been in the toilet for a very long time, and they were worried.

I knocked on the toilet door, but there was no response. I unlocked the door manually, and upon opening it, the passenger fell out into the cabin, unconscious. My crew panicked. I immediately went for help and to get the defibrillator. We did CPR for an hour but ultimately accepted that our passenger had died. We moved the body into a body bag and placed her by the back door. Then I woke my sleeping teammates. We still had seven hours left on the flight.

This isn't the kind of experience you can be prepared for, no matter how much training you go through. But I learned that day that I was the kind of person who can manage that kind of challenge.

Sometimes we get to say what kind of person we are, and sometimes we discover it.

What kind of person are you to yourself? And what kind of person are you to those around you?

2

WHY ARE YOU HERE?

Why are you working at your current company and not somewhere else? I work at IntrepidAir because I need a salary to support my kids, I am saving for my retirement as I have lived outside of the country I was born in for over twenty years and will not be entitled to an pension, and oh, I absolutely *love* the travel benefits. I fly a lot, and if I were to pay full fare, I would have to earn a lot more money than I do now.

Did you know that in the U.S. the average amount of time a 25–34-year-old stays in a company is only 2.8 years and that for people working in service occupations it's just 1.9 years?[3] That's not a lot of time. So why do people take certain jobs? And why do they stay in them? And why doesn't the average young employee last more than 1.9 years in their service industry job?

And what about you? No one's looking. No one can hear you. What are your goals in life? What are you currently trying to achieve? Why are you in your current role?

I bet that no matter what your reason, it has little or nothing to do with your company's products or services. This is true of nearly everyone, in nearly every company. And that's fine. But you're participating in your economic community because doing so is leading you to achieve your personal goals. By being at IntrepidAir I am achieving my goal of earning enough money to support my kids, save for my retirement and travel.

You're in your role because it's the best way you know to go forward. Your job is the direct result of your free will. Every decision you have ever made has led you here, to this role. You could be somewhere else, doing something else. There are a thousand other places you could be if you think about the path you have traveled in life, and the opportunities you didn't take. But you're not in any of those other places. You are where you are. That's not to say, "it is what it is," but rather, "it is what you made it."

---

3   U.S. Bureau of Labour Statistics. 2020. Employee Tenure in 2020. Retrieved from https://www.bls.gov/news.release/pdf/tenure.pdf

So why are you in your job? Because this is the fastest and most effective way you know of for you to reach your personal goals. Because if you were aware of a faster or more effective way, you would be doing that instead. You're smarter than that.

And why do you think you are here and not someone else?

Your company isn't made of idiots either.

At IntrepidAir, we hire roughly a quarter of the people we interview for cabin crew. That means for everyone in our inflight services department, we talked to twenty people, ten of them probably could have done the job, and we picked five to join us. Why do you think that is? Why did we pick one person and not another?

And on that note, why were you selected for your job instead of someone else?

Your experience perhaps? Your education? The charity work you did on the side in high school? The layout of your CV? The extra course in excel mastery?

Look, those things got you to the interview, but the truth is it's your character that got you the job. You were the kind of person they were looking for. Interviewers aren't idiots. They don't waste their time interviewing anyone who isn't already qualified for the job. If you weren't qualified, you wouldn't have been invited to the interview. It wasn't your qualifications that got you the job. It was who you were in the interview.

Companies are organizations of humans, and humans want people that fit into the culture of the organization they are building. You are not in your job because of your education, experience, or skills, those are the reasons they talked to you. The reason they chose you is that you are a kind of person.

Now think of the people you work with and describe what kind of people your community consistently chooses? What are the kinds of people that you employ at your company?

You might describe the kinds of people in your organization as caring, loving, kind, supporting, and empathetic, which I find to be especially true of the kinds of people that work in the medical field. Or you might say that your company hires the kinds of people that are driven, hardworking, self-motivated, and powerful, as I see when I talk to people in financial services. Or you might describe your company as filled with the kinds of people that are thoughtful, agile, outgoing, and quality conscious, as I find most people in the high-scale restaurant industry to be.

Or you may describe the kinds of people you work with as sneaky, selfish, underhanded, and mean. Or as apathetic, lazy, cowardly, and weak. But be careful, if you describe everyone around you in negative terms, guess what? You were chosen because you were a "good fit" too. If you think that everyone around you is a certain kind of person and that culture experts from that community looking for a "good fit" chose you by mistake, you're highly likely to be gravely mistaken. You'll need to live with that. People tend to pick people for their teams who are "like them."

I want you to come up with five words that describe the people that work at your company. Not just those on your team... the entire company.

_____

_____

_____

Do you notice something about these words? None of those are on anyone's CVs. You don't say, "I'm diverse" or, "I'm human" on your CV.

A football team isn't assembled based on the skill or experience of the players. Players are considered for the team based on those things, and they're invited to try out. A tryout is a time when managers, owners, and coaches get to see if a skilled and experienced player is also a "good fit" for the team. Do they pass instead of taking a risky shot? Do they encourage their teammates when things don't go well? Are they fun to play with, and helpful to those around them? Can they suppress their ego when the team needs them to? Do they continue to train hard when they think no one is looking? If you want a skilled and experienced player, read their CV. But if you want a strong team, skills and experience won't provide nearly enough information.

Like any other organization, yours is a team of people who get together every day to play a particular economic game. You might be in the restaurant game, the tire manufacturing game, the medical waste disposal game, or the microchip sales game. I'm in the aviation game. In my game, I'm building a team to play the game with me, and I want certain kinds of people on my team. If my team works well together, our team will win the aviation game together, and if we don't play together well, we lose together too. But it starts with having a certain kind of player on my team because we're a certain kind of team in a certain kind of game.

So, to recap, your work isn't just your job, it's your life. Your company is a team of people playing an economic game so you can all achieve your personal goals together. Therefore, you need certain kinds of people to play the game well. And you were chosen because you're that kind of person.

Improving quality of life

All teams, in all games, are looking for players who improve the quality of life for the others on their teams. When I met my husband, I discovered pretty quickly that he was the kind of person that I wanted on my life team, but it wasn't because of his CV. It wasn't because he was successful, it was because he actively pursued my success. It wasn't because he was described as kind, it was because I experienced kindness from him. It wasn't because people called him inspirational, it was because he inspired me. And it wasn't because he was just supportive, but because he actively did things to improve the quality of my life. Relentlessly. He entered my life as a wellspring of unsolicited daily encouragement and activities that showed me those things in real-time. Who he said he was didn't change my life. What came out through his hands and feet, that's what made a difference.

It wasn't long after we met that I noticed changes in my own behavior as well. When you are consistently encouraged, supported, and served, it's tough to hold all of that in without reflecting it on others around you. Being helpful is infectious. I naturally began to behave differently as well. My cynicism about my job melted away, and I started seeing my colleagues as people whose lives I could improve each day. I even began to see myself as someone I was responsible for helping. It was like the universe had done me a favor, and I was compelled to return it in kind.

Now you might be starting to see how you have the power to make and improve the quality of your life and the lives of those around you. What are some of the things you can do to bring joy into the half of your life that you are spending together with your colleagues at work?

Come up with a list of things you can do that make you and your team happy, that help you bond with each other, etc. Make two lists – one you can do in your everyday personal life and another you can do when you are working. Here are some quick examples to get you started:

- Patting someone on the back
- Opening the door for them when you walk into the office
- Nominate someone for employee of the month
- Bring food to work to share with your team
- Make a card for a team member's birthday and sing happy birthday
- Help someone study for their accreditation exams
- Pick something up that someone has dropped
- Tell them not to worry about their mistake
- Make someone a coffee
- Deliver some compliments
- Use peoples' names
- Help someone carry their bag up or down the stairs

Now it's your turn. Just come up with five small things you can do starting from tomorrow that would improve the quality of work-life for you and your colleagues:

1. _____

2. _____

3. _____

4. _____

5. _____

What do you notice about the things that you have written down? They are all activities, not one of them is a hope or an intention. They are all activities. They are all actions. They must be executed to be meaningful. Do you know why?

Your intentions do not matter, only your actions and words matter. And your actions and words will entice others to act. It is infectious. As a customer service agent in your team, you have the opportunity to infect not only your team but all of your customers as well. I want you to think about that next time you have an intention and think about doing something. Your intentions are only meaningful to you. Everyone else judges you by your words and actions. That's all they have to go on. So, act on that intention to make an impact. Be the kind of person that puts thoughts into action.

Here's the thing, your brain rewards you for doing things with a neurochemical called dopamine. You get a hit of dopamine every time you get something done. But the odd part is that you actually get a hit of dopamine just for thinking about getting something done as well. This is why it's pleasurable for you to put items into your cart on Amazon, even if you don't buy them. Your brain rewards you for your intention to buy them by giving you a hit of the most addictive and pleasurable chemical on the planet.

So, if you're thinking of doing something nice for someone, or helping someone out, or saying something encouraging to someone, or giving someone a nice gift, your brain will reward you just for thinking about it. The problem is that you haven't actually done anything for anyone. You've consumed the reward without earning it. So, you can be easily self-deceived into thinking that you've done something meaningful when you haven't done anything at all. Your intentions will only matter to you, and your intentions will be pleasurable and addictive even if you never do anything about them.

So, we're all walking around making ourselves feel good and not putting our intentions into action. It's like a kind of awkward, mental self-pleasuring trick. It's only ever going to be valuable to you, and you'll never get the credit you deserve for that intention because no one else will ever experience it. Only you will know how good-hearted you actually are.

If you've ever wondered why people think of you as less caring than you actually are, this is probably why. You're most often the only person who's experienced your care, even if it's for other people. You've felt care, but not expressed it, and you've rewarded yourself for it.

So, here's what you do. Be the kind of person who puts your intentions into action. If you're thinking about calling a friend and checking up on them because you haven't heard from them in a week, then do it. If now is not the best time, then use your tools. Set an alarm on your phone to make sure that you bring this intention into action in the future.

We've all got mobile phones. Mine is full of reminders, alarms, and calendar appointments, all set to remind me at better times to drag an intention that I had at some point, into reality. Right now, I have a reminder on my phone to call a friend of mine from Australia this coming Saturday, because I thought about it yesterday, and I'm going to forget if I don't write it down. Make an alarm.

Whenever one of my crew members experiences a significant event, like a death in the family, I put a reminder in my calendar to send them a follow-up WhatsApp message in a few days, to make sure they're okay. I have thousands of crew, and it would be impossible for me to remember to do all of those things if I didn't use my resources to help me.

Intentions aren't valuable without actions, and it's the same in reverse. You can't act unless there's an intention. In order to accomplish anything, you have to want to accomplish it. And for that, you need to know what you want.

3

WHAT DO YOU WANT?

My father-in-law worked for 35 years in the same company. He started and ended his career in the same company. He never had the need for something else, or if he did, he never pursued it. He had a good paycheck, job satisfaction, and a decent boss. His annual reviews were enough for him to know where he could improve on his weaknesses, and that gave him enough insight to allow him to adapt well enough to keep his job. That's what he wanted from his job, a job. But that's not what people want now.

What do you really think people want out of a job?

The most extensive study of this subject in the world was conducted by Gallup across 50,000 business units covering 47 industries and twenty years of data including 1.4 million employees. They found that what we thought people were looking for in a job (the past, our parents), and what they are *actually* looking for (the present, us), are very different.

We thought people wanted money, we thought people wanted just to be satisfied in their jobs, we thought people wanted a good boss who gave annual reviews, focusing on their weaknesses so they would know where they can do better, and we thought people looked at their job as 'just a job'. We thought most people were still like my father-in-law.

We were completely wrong. Times have changed.

The study found that instead of a paycheck what people actually want is purpose. Yes, there needs to be a paycheck, but it doesn't replace the need for people to be fulfilling their personal purpose. I know this is true for myself as well. Yes, I need a salary, but if I was offered twice what I'm making to work in a job where I wouldn't be happy, I just couldn't do it. It's not all about money.

Instead of job satisfaction, we discovered that people want continuous development. And because they want development instead of a good boss, they are looking for a manager/coach who will provide feedback that focuses on their strengths through ongoing conversations. No one is willing to wait for a year-end review anymore. This trend continued:[4]

What people used to want	What they want now
Paycheck	Purpose
Satisfaction	Development
Boss	Coach
Annual Review	Ongoing Conversations
Weaknesses	Strengths
Job	Life

With all of this change in the motivations of people, it's no wonder people are spending less time in their jobs. Especially in the service industry, which tends to be behind on employee experience design and aligning jobs with real motivations. How differently would your company have to run if the management were to pay attention to the items on the right in the table above? And what would happen to that 1.9-year average tenure in the service industry if restaurants, airlines, barber shops, cleaning companies, and hotels started to organize themselves on the principles of purpose, development, coaching, conversation, strengths, and life? Would people find greater connections and community in customer service?

Studies show that people don't enjoy their jobs as much as they enjoy their co-workers. People don't care nearly as much about

---

4   Clifton, J., J. Harter. (2019) It's the Manager. Gallup Press, USA.

what they're doing as they do about why they're doing it and who they're doing it with. People who enjoy working with the people they work with, last longer in their companies, are higher performing, and more productive. That's a good deal for the company.

The same Gallup study cited above found that companies whose employees were more engaged at work experienced:

1. 41% lower absenteeism
2. 59% less turnover
3. 28% less shrinkage
4. 70% fewer safety incidents (which, in aviation is a pretty big deal)
5. 40% fewer defects
6. 10% better customer ratings
7. 17% higher productivity
8. 20% higher sales
9. 21% higher profitability[5]

So, it looks like from the employer standpoint, it's a no-brainer. You really want your people to be engaged in work they find meaningful. But what about the employee experience? Surely with greater profitability, performance, and productivity, the employees must not be having a good time, right? Maybe that extra profit comes from salary reductions?

---

5   Clifton, J., J. Harter. (2019) It's the Manager. Gallup Press, USA.

Nope.

In truth, people really want to be in the kind of work where they perform better and make more profit for their companies. A study by BetterUp (2017) showed that 90% of people are willing to work for 23% less if they are working in a job that they enjoy, and with people they like.[6] Not 23% less on their current salary, but 23% fewer lifetime earnings! That's huge! Seeing as the average person only spends 21% of their income on housing, that makes meaningful work more valuable than shelter from a priority perspective. People really value this stuff.

But it's not like employees have to sacrifice earnings in order to find meaning in their jobs. They are willing to, but they don't have to. In fact, people who find more meaning at work tend to perform better and get along with their colleagues better, which leads to more opportunities for advancement and higher salaries. So, the irony is, people who find meaning in their jobs are willing to work for less but will actually get paid more.

It's not all about the money either. People who find meaning at work live more meaningful lives. Studies have shown that people who live more meaningful lives, live longer lives as well.[7] That's right folks, if we get this right, employees will make more

6   BetterUp. (2017) Meaning and Purpose at Work. USA
7   Steger, Michael. What Makes Life Meaningful: Michael Steger at TEDxCSU. https://www.youtube.com/watch?v=RLFVoEF2RIo

money and live longer lives, and companies will make more money and live longer lives too.

Remember our discussion above about how IntrepidAir survived the 2018–2021 period without a single forced redundancy?

Yep. That's how we did it. We helped each other find meaning in what we were doing together, and we all played our part in making sure our economic community would survive the crisis.

In training programs, I commonly ask my teammates, why does it matter that they are cabin crew? What meaningful service are they providing? Why does them being here matter?

Is it important?
Is it significant?
Is it relevant?

In the airline industry, it's easy to find meaning in these questions. Think about this from the perspective of a member of my cabin crew – you don't know the context for why people are flying, but what you do know is that the people who are flying aren't doing it on a whim, they are doing it for a reason.

In fact, 80% of our passengers in economy fly for leisure. It might be for a vacation, a weekend getaway with a new lover, or to check off a bucket-list destination that they've been saving up to see in real life. They might be traveling to attend a funeral and console their bereaved family. Or perhaps they are attending their sister's wedding, and they finally get to meet her fiancé for the first time. Or maybe it's to attend the birth of a nephew or niece, or if a man has been working away from his family, to meet his own newborn child for the very first time. Or they could be going to a new job, or maybe they just lost a job and they are returning home to start a new chapter.

Nine times out of ten people are in a position of either traveling for something 'good' or traveling for something 'bad', because traveling on a plane on a Friday isn't something people do for fun. No matter where they are going or coming from, it is an event for them, and it is probably the kind of event they take pictures of, the kind of event they write home about, and the kind of event they post on social media. People don't remember much about the content of their experience, but they do remember how they felt.

So, each member of my crew is contributing to one of the defining moments of that passenger's year, or maybe even their life. No one gets onboard because they are bored. They are there to get somewhere special. It is probably one of the more meaningful moments of their year or life. It is not like taking a trip to the grocery store.

Cabin crew are in a job where they become a part of a significant experience for every single passenger they interact with. It's a bit like being a server in a restaurant, surrounded by business deals being forged, romances blossoming, or friendships deepening all around you. Or like nurses in a hospital, surrounded by loved ones in pain, cancer patients clinging to hope, and newborns beginning their lives.

What cabin crew are doing onboard is meaningful because what their passengers are doing is meaningful. That passenger has invited our crew member into a meaningful moment in their life. You too get to choose what 'kind of person' you want to be, and how you can have an impact on a person's meaningful moment in your service.

In December 2019 I had to fly home for a family emergency. My mum had a heart attack and was going into open-heart surgery. I was on a plane to Melbourne within nine hours of finding out this information. I was emotional, I hadn't eaten in about twelve hours, and I had all the worst thoughts running through my head.

As I boarded the aircraft a crew member who was standing near my seat welcomed me onboard and asked if I was going home for Christmas. I told him no. Then he asked if I was going on a holiday. I told him no I was traveling for a family emergency and asked him not to ask me about it as I might cry.

He told me he was sorry to hear that, he then introduced himself by name and told me if I needed anything during the flight to just ask him. He then left me to settle into my seat. About five minutes later he brought me a small bottle of water and an extra pillow. I of course thanked him and told him he was very kind. He said to me, "It is really hard being away from family, especially in times like these, and I'm sorry you are traveling alone, but I am here if you want to talk and pass the time after the service."

I was extremely touched by this, here was a guy in his thirties, who didn't even know me, reaching out to me because he genuinely cared.

He was the kind of person who could recognize that I was not in a good way and although he couldn't take away how I was feeling, he recognized that he could make my journey as comfortable as possible.

He then asked where I lived, and I told him I lived in Dubai and went on to say I had rushed home from work, packed my bags and I actually hadn't even eaten anything since breakfast (it was now 9 pm).

We made some more small talk before he had to carry on with assisting other passengers. As we were taxiing out for takeoff, he came to me and discreetly gave me a packet of nuts and said, "Hopefully this will hold you off until after takeoff and we serve your meal."

Now this crew member did not know I worked for IntrepidAir, or that I had been in the aviation industry for twenty years. That didn't matter, because he was the kind of person who treated people the way he would want to be treated, or how he would want someone else to treat his friends and family in the same position as I was in.

He made an impact on me during that meaningful moment in my life. I have told many people about this, and I even wrote to the airline about how he made me feel. Remember, people forget what we do and what we say, but they remember how we made them feel. How do you want people to feel around you? And how does creating that experience for them help you to reach your goals?

In order to get what you want, are you willing to change yourself? And are you willing to make changes to who you are in your corporate community?

Write down one thing you would like to change in the way you approach your employee experience at work. This could be anything, even simple changes, such as:

- I would like to speak better about people
- I would like to utilize my time in my job more intentionally as a career step
- I would like to behave in a way that makes others view me as more of a leader

The one thing I would like to change in my employee experience is...

_____

_____

_____

Now, using a minimum of three examples of things you would like to change, I want you to write down what kind of person you want to be at work. For starters, you can complete this sentence: "I want to be the kind of person who..."

Now be honest, the more honest you are the more you will get out of this exercise. And think carefully because this is something that you might decide to share with your boss during your next meeting, and something you will work towards during your tenure in your current role.

You may already be the kind of person you want to be, and that is fine. If that's the case, write down what kind of person you are.

1. _____

2. _____

3. _____

4. _____

5. _____

Thank you for your honesty in this exercise. I don't want you to just read a book about customer service, I want you to actually find meaning in the role, and this is an important step for you in doing so.

4

SERVICE ATTITUDE

I've been on the receiving end of a few great customer service experiences. For example, I went on a weekend getaway with my husband to the Maldives in 2018.

Now all the resorts in the Maldives are pretty much the same: pristine blue waters, beaches that wrap around the resort, the whole cast of Finding Nemo out among the corals each day. But the award-winning differentiator for me was a Sri Lankan concierge named Taj. He was in his late twenties, tall and thin with magical white teeth. As we got off our two-hour seaplane journey, he was on the jetty waiting for us. He greeted us with his magical smile and said, "Welcome Mr & Mrs Block, my name is Taj and I will be looking after you during your stay."

Wait ... what? He knew our names ... woooooooooo! We later realized there were only three couples on the plane and they had copies of our passports. But wow they took the time to know us before we even got to the island.

So, he arranged our bags to be taken from the jetty to our rooms whilst he took us to the bar area where he checked us in, he told us all about the resort and informed us if we needed anything arranging – meals, activities, spa sessions – he would arrange it all for us. He dropped us at our gorgeous beach villa and he disappeared. But disappearing wasn't his talent, reappearing out of the blue was.

Throughout the four days, Taj would just randomly appear at the strangest moments. At breakfast, whilst we were sitting at the pool, or grabbing an ice cream at the ice cream parlor. He would ask if everything was okay, engage in polite conversation, and ask if he could assist us in booking anything.

One afternoon we decided to make the trek around the island which takes around 90 minutes. We were walking along the beach at the far end of the island when he suddenly, popped up again out of the jungle with a massive grin on his face and asked, "How are you both today Mr and Mrs Block?". He wanted to make sure we booked our free spa treatment before it got all booked up. Which of course we had forgotten about and so we booked it. We then joked with him about how he found us, and if there was a GPS tracker we didn't know about that he could see on his tablet. We asked him how he knew where we were all the time, and do you know what he said? "It's my job to know."

Right through our entire stay, Taj was always there when we needed him, effortlessly taking care of us. The day we departed he arranged everything for us, told us our seaplane was at 3 pm and to just go and sit in the outside bar and he would come to get us. The seaplane was running an hour late and he came past to let us know and told us not to worry that he would come and get us when it was time. And he did just that. When we boarded the plane, he helped us and we thanked him for our stay. As the plane taxied out for takeoff, we looked out the window, and while taking off we could still see Taj standing on the jetty waving to us with that big magical smile on his face.

It then occurred to me that he really was a miracle. He was the kind of person who obviously found meaning in his work and that his work was a large part of his meaningful life.

We have already talked about how when passengers buy a ticket with IntrepidAir they are inviting our crew to be a part of a meaningful event in their life. The type of event they tell their friends about, write on social media, and take pictures of. Remember people don't remember much about what happened or what was said, they remember how they felt.

When I booked that hotel in the Maldives, I was inviting Taj into a meaningful moment in my life, the type I took lots of pictures of, the type I definitely bragged about on social media, and the type I tell people about over and over again.

You have a choice to be the kind of person who connects with your customers, just like Taj connected with me. Connecting with your customers will give you the greatest chance of them returning again.

If I went back to the Maldives, I would have to stay in Taj's hotel again, I would feel like I was cheating on him if I didn't!

Why are you in your customer service role? Well, probably for reasons that have nothing to do with your company, your brand, or maybe even your services. But you know that being there is your best route to success because you're not an idiot. You wouldn't be there if you could be achieving your personal goals better somewhere else. So, since this is your best chance at success, wouldn't you want to give it your best effort? Wouldn't you want to know that you were doing it in the right way as well? What's your service attitude?

Service attitudes

I have identified and highlighted four different kinds of service attitudes. Let's go through them together and try to identify which of these is your dominant attitude toward your work each day.

It's not my responsibility	Nothing is too much trouble
I'm just doing my job and nothing more	I know what needs doing so let's get on with it and get it done.

ACTIVE

PASSIVE

AVOIDANCE   ACCEPTANCE

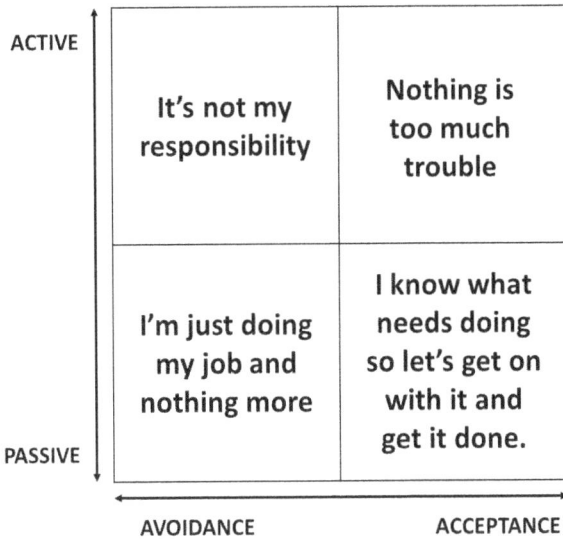

1. ACTIVE AVOIDANCE

Narrative: It's not my responsibility

Sometimes customer service staff can appear as though they don't even want to be there. They may be perceived as uncaring. They might even intentionally or unintentionally ignore their customers and can often appear as unwelcoming or indifferent.

It really gets under my skin when I board a flight to find out that the inflight entertainment isn't working at my seat. If it's a full flight, that means I'm likely to be the only passenger sentenced to spend the entire flight without access to the movies and music that the others are enjoying around me.

This happened to me on a flight I took recently, not on IntrepidAir (although it's probably fair to let you know that this sometimes happens on our flights too. Technology is not always as cooperative as we would like it to be). Anyway, I mentioned to the crew member that my inflight entertainment system wasn't working, and do you know what he said?

"It isn't my fault. But you can send an email to our complaint department if you want."

Wow.

I mean.

Just wow.

Now, this guy couldn't have known who I was in the industry, or that his words to me would be recorded as an immortal example of exactly how NOT to deal with customers, but still, he could have done much better. Maybe he was having an off day.

How do you think that response made me feel?

I immediately lost confidence in that crew member and sacrificed a bit of respect for the company as a whole. I was angry that I was not taken seriously and passed from one person to another. I was frustrated because on top of feeling like I wasn't getting what I had paid for, I was also betrayed by the person I had counted on to try and mitigate that unmet expectation.

Is that you? Or do you have days like that? Be honest with yourself. Do you ever pass customers off, or ignore or dismiss their complaints?

So, what could that wayward crew member have said to me instead?

"Oh, I know Madam, we are having so much trouble with the inflight entertainment today, you must be so frustrated, let me see if I can reset the system and I'll come back to you in ten minutes."

He could have said this even if he knew there was no system to reset. Or that the system had already been reset in a previous attempt to address this issue.

How might I have felt in that case?

Even if he couldn't fix it, I would have known that he cared and that he was willing to take the time and try to fix the problem! That's generally all someone wants. Think about yourself – you want someone to care about you, to take the time to listen to you, and to try and fix the problem.

I've already taught my cabin crew that using the phrase, "send an email to our complaint department," without having already made a significant attempt at trying to solve the problem, is not an acceptable level of service.

If you think of yourself as the customer of your manager, and after you raise an issue your manager replies to you, "If you don't like it, send an email to the Human Resources department," how would you feel? Perhaps just as frustrated and betrayed as I did. You are your manager's customer. And you are the service provider for your customers.

You have the power to be the kind of person who actively avoids inviting customers to complain to anyone other than you. You can stop the complaint where you are by taking responsibility for being the person who will exhaust all available options for trying to set it right for your customer.

2. PASSIVE AVOIDANCE

Narrative: I am just doing my job and nothing more

Customer service professionals can come across as uncaring or unhelpful, not because they are avoiding responsibility, but because they feel like it isn't their responsibility to begin with. They will generally do something if it falls within what they think they are expected to do, but they won't go out of their way to help or use initiative to go beyond the borders of their job descriptions. This can happen if a customer service professional feels disempowered or marginalized at work. They feel that if no one in their company is willing to go the extra mile for them, then why should they do so for their customers. I understand that frustration, but the customer shouldn't be punished for the mistakes of the company's poor treatment of their employees.

I recently left a necklace in a hotel when I was traveling. Now, it wasn't a particularly valuable necklace, but it was one of my favorites, so I decided to try and track it down once I got home. I called the reception and told them my name and the room I had checked out of a couple of days before. I explained that I thought I had left my necklace in my room and was told, "Sorry, Ma'am. That's not my department, you'll need to talk to security, would you like me to connect you?"

Now, all of that may be true, and I understand that the receptionist was trying to be a little bit helpful without going out of her way to do so, but it wouldn't have been that difficult for her to ask me for a brief description of the necklace and offer to call me back. It would have saved me the next two exchanges.

I accepted the connection with the security office and after telling the officer what my necklace looked like he replied, "Ya, we don't have anything like that here. You should call housekeeping, hang on, I'll transfer you."

Again, perhaps it's true that housekeeping might have it, and that it's not the security officer's job to track down my necklace, but seriously, how hard is it for him to have made that call on my behalf to limit the number of people I would need to talk to.

I waited on the line for housekeeping for a full minute, which in customer experience terms might as well be a week. A lady picked up the phone who didn't speak much English. I struggled to communicate with her. I gave her a description of my necklace only out of the purist form of optimism that she would understand any of it, to which she replied, "No. No have. No having that one. Sorry. Thank you."

And that was it. I gave up.

Had the receptionist I first called taken down the description and made the calls, she could have eliminated the call with security for me and spoken in Spanish to the housekeeping office. Perhaps with those conversations happening in the hotel's native language, a memory might have been sparked and my necklace located… but instead, I let go of something of mine that I really liked, in order to avoid any more of the customer relationship experience necessary to dig any deeper than I already had. I was very disappointed.

I told you at the beginning of this book that 91% of customers who have a complaint won't tell the company, but they will tell fifteen other people… and I am no exception. I didn't bother calling again. And I won't bother visiting them again. And most of my friends will probably avoid that hotel on their vacations now. What a tragedy.

Sometimes you will have the opportunity to provide a level of service that goes beyond the edges of your job description. It's your choice to show that you care and are willing to be helpful. I've also had the privilege of being on the receiving end of customer service experiences where I know that my server has gone above and beyond the norm for their role. And I have rewarded those servers with tips, those companies with loyalty, and with praise to my same group of friends.

As your manager's customer, how would you feel if you ask them for something and they reply to you, "that's not my department," or "that's not my problem?" How would you feel? Maybe you've felt that in your role. Your manager might be accurate in what they're saying, but they're missing out on an opportunity to go above and beyond their role in their service to you as well. And you will likely respond like any customer would, by not giving them feedback, but instead by complaining to fifteen other people about how badly treated you are at work.

Be the kind of person who is willing to move outside of your specific role and responsibilities in order to achieve a good customer service experience. Your customer will notice and appreciate it. They will reward you with loyalty and by sending their friends to you as well, if not by also leaving you a good tip.

3. PASSIVE ACCEPTANCE

Narrative: I know what needs doing so let's get on with it and get it done.

These customer service professionals actually get done what needs to be done, but they're not happy about it, and they'll often let you know. They approach customer service as transactional and tend not to move beyond indifference to the customer experience. The services they provide will get done, and probably quickly, but in a rush and with minimal interaction with their customers.

My husband and I had an experience like this at a restaurant in Dubai recently. My husband likes his steak medium-rare. Now, he's not a particularly picky eater, but if you ask him how he wants his steak, and you bring it to him cooked medium-well instead of medium-rare, he'll tell you.

The waiter was visibly annoyed. He tried to tell my husband that the steak was actually medium rare when in fact it wasn't. That's a hard mistake to make in an upscale restaurant. The waiter wanted to avoid having to correct the error. Perhaps it was to avoid a potential conflict with the chef, to avoid the embarrassment of having to admit that he had entered the order incorrectly in the system, or to avoid the expense of cooking a new steak since steaks can't be made rarer once they're overcooked. In any case, he pursed his lips, grimaced a little, and responded,

"Well sir, this is how we normally serve our steaks."

To which my husband replied, "Well sir, then you shouldn't have asked me how I wanted it served."

So, the waiter took a deep breath, explained that it will take some time, but that he will bring a new steak as soon as possible.

It wasn't as soon as possible, but it was correctly cooked the second time around. The waiter also avoided us for the rest of our meal. We didn't get the common inquiries about the quality of our food, or if we would like anything else. We skipped dessert, asked for the bill, and never went back.

It's important to note here that from a transactional standpoint, we received exactly what we ordered in the end. A mistake was made and corrected. The issue here isn't the lack of delivery, it's the lack of empathy in that delivery. My husband and I were made to feel like we had done something wrong in asking for the meal to be corrected. But what we wanted was exactly what we had ordered. Sometimes the only missing ingredient in an otherwise good customer experience is attitude.

Be honest with yourself now, have you ever given one of your customers the impression that you are going out of your way to help them and that they should recognize how inconvenient that service is for you to execute? That's a more subtle form of disdain for your customer than outright refusal to be helpful. You might justify to yourself that since your customer got what they wanted, your attitude was immaterial to the transaction.

You got it done in the end, so why should it matter if you were happy about it during the process? Well, because we never went back to that restaurant, that's why. And now I'm writing about it in my book as an example of what NOT to do. Just as important as what you do is how you do it, and your attitude makes a huge difference in the customer's experience of your service, even if you do go out of your way.

Be the kind of person that gets it done, with a smile.

4. ACTIVE ACCEPTANCE

Narrative: Nothing is too much trouble

In this attitude, the service provider uses their initiative to not only anticipate customer needs but does things the customers didn't even think they wanted! They come across as natural, responsive, caring, real, and understanding. They go out of their way to make sure that each of their customers are cared for and deliver delightful experiences when they can.

My husband recently bought a new car, so he took his old one in to be serviced ahead of selling it. The service center did a full interior and exterior detailing and changed the front windshield because it had a crack in it. Now, it was a seven-year-old car, so a bit of wear and tear is expected, but the quality of the service he received was really not amazing. After receiving the car back, he sent a WhatsApp video to the garage manager, to show him that the door wells and cup holders weren't wiped out, and there was some frayed material on the front seat that could have been trimmed but was neglected.

The manager immediately rang my husband back. Knowing that 91% of customers with a complaint won't say anything, the manager was keen to take advantage of this rare opportunity for improvement. He offered to pick up and drop off the car by truck, but my husband insisted on driving it back into the garage himself. The manager listened as my husband walked him through the car and showed him what a customer is likely to notice that a mechanic might not. In the end, the garage redid the interior and exterior detailing, and to my husband's delight, repainted the front bumper at no extra cost, and delivered the car back to us by truck.

For sure that was a loss for the garage, right? Or was it?

If only one out of ten customers with a complaint will tell you and each of them tell fifteen other people about their complaint, my husband's complaint indicated to the garage manager that there were likely more than 135 potential customers in the market that were already aware of the quality control gap and would not likely use this garage's services as a result. If you were the manager, how much would it be worth for you to get those 135 potential customers back?

Yes. It wasn't a cost for the manager to fix the problem, it was an investment. My husband helped the garage to build in a sanity check to their quality control process, to make sure that vehicles were given a quick review by someone, not on the team attending to the car, but pretending to be the owner before the car left the garage.

This bad customer service experience is an example in a book on customer service, about how to do it right. This is what you should be striving for in the case of a complaint. But more than this, you should strive to get it right before a complaint can ever develop.

You should be Taj.

Taj didn't have to turn around any part of his customer service for my husband and I on our vacation to the Maldives. He was perfect, but more than perfect, because he anticipated things we might want and provided the opportunity before we even had a chance to ask for them. That's a great active acceptance attitude.

Now think back on your customer service attitude over the last three months. Perhaps you've exhibited all four at some point, but one of them will be your dominant behavior. Be honest with yourself. Which service attitude do you exhibit most of the time?

If you consistently identify with 1, 2, or 3, then you have work to do to get to a 4. A 4 is where you <u>MUST</u> be.

Now I am going to be honest with you… I am not a #4 100% of the time, that is impossible. And keep in mind that I'm the one who wrote the book on customer service (the one you're reading right now). I am still human. But if I had to put a number on it, I'd say I am a #4 about 93.5% of the time. Oddly specific perhaps, but I really did think about it a lot, and I took into consideration all the feedback I receive from my crew as well.

Customer service is an attitude, NOT a department.

Depending on your industry, it can take months or even years for your company to attract a new customer. The cost of acquisition for a new customer is high, especially in competitive industries. After the marketing department has fought hard on your behalf to bring that customer to you so you can show them what you're made of… you can lose that customer in seconds if you have the wrong service attitude.

Remember, the customer is the arbiter that decides where the money goes. They are the one that either brings the money to your team, so you can share it around and feed your families and educate your kids… or they will bring that money to your competitor's team, and their kids will be educated and families fed. Think about it. People have been competing on economic teams for a long time. The team that's winning gets more of the money, and their families benefit. You're the front line in that competition.

The accountants, marketing team, delivery drivers, human resource managers, secretaries, and graphic designers in your company won't interact with customers, so if they want their families fed and children educated, they have to rely on you to bring that money in. They're trusting you to provide an amazing quality of service to your shared customers so that all of you will have enough resources to share among your families. In return, they supply support services for you, like marketing, manufacturing, recruiting, planning, logistics, and leadership.

The customer must be at the center of everything you do, without them there is no company. Simple fact. YOU are your company's differentiator against all the other companies in your industry. It's you.

Have you ever stopped going somewhere because of the service? What happened?

In general, it is customer service that will keep a customer or drive them away. We all know this because we have all done it. We have all not gone back to an establishment because of the poor customer service.

What is the key differentiator between great service (service attitude 4) and average service and inconsistent service (service attitudes 2 and 3)?

It is your personal attitude.

It's not rocket science. Customers continue to go where they are treated well and avoid places where they have a less enjoyable experience. And as much as your product or service matters, your attitude matters more. Customers will turn away a great product or service if the attitude of the service provider isn't in line with their expectations.

Your attitude is a combination of your thoughts and feelings, and it comes out and is exhibited to the world through your behaviors, including the tone and pace of your voice, the position of your eyebrows, and the movement of your hands. Your behavior is the natural expression of your attitude; your attitude is most dramatically and consistently influenced by your default mindset.

5

MINDSET

It was just a bad day. Miriam forgot to set her alarm and woke up late. "Oh great!" she thought, "this is just what I need today." She rushed to get herself ready for the day. Tripping through her morning routine with a bit of panic in each step, she ended up poking herself in the eye with her mascara and spilling coffee on her shirt. She swore her way out of the bathroom and back to the closet. On her way to the mall, a song came on the radio that reminded her of her ex-boyfriend. She thought of what a jerk he was and how she's better off without him. But why *that* song? And why today? Certainly, the universe must be against her, so she was already on the defensive by the time she got to work.

"Glad you could join us," her boss said, as he glanced at his watch to see she was just barely running in on time. He was smiling. "Whatever," she smirked sarcastically back at him. She reminded herself of what an idiot her boss was and how she had decided not to pay attention to his snarky comments anymore. The electronics store was already buzzing with the first few customers as she took her place behind the customer service desk to greet her first angry customer of the day.

"This robot vacuum is the stupidest thing I've ever bought! I want a refund."

"What's that smell?" replied Miriam.

The customer yelled back, "I was at work yesterday and my dog crapped on the floor and this stupid thing spent the rest of the day smearing it all over the carpet."

She knew she was supposed to smile politely and be helpful, but honestly, what did this guy think would happen? Miriam considered her words carefully and forced a polite smile.

"Don't yell at me, it's not my fault. Plus, it sounds to me like the product performed exactly as it should. It's not broken. And you bought it more than a month ago, so I can't give you a refund. Have a nice day and thank you for shopping at Gadgets."

"It figures," thought Miriam... "Just a bad start to another bad day."

But what if...

It was just a good day?

Miriam forgot to set her alarm and woke up late. "Oh great!" she thought, "a few extra minutes of sleep is just what I needed today." She rushed to get herself ready for the day. Singing her favorite song through her morning routine helped her move a little quicker than normal, and she even had time to sit down for a cup of coffee before she left the house. On her way to the mall, a song came on the radio that reminded her of her ex-boyfriend. She thought about her ex and wondered if he was doing as well as she was. But why *that* song? And why today? Certainly, the universe must be telling her something, so she expressed her gratitude for what she's learned from that relationship and remained in that attitude when she got to work.

"Glad you could join us," her boss said, as he glanced at his watch to see she was just barely running in on time. He was smiling. "Me too!" she said gleefully as she smiled back at him. She reminded herself of how attentive her boss was and how she had decided to try to learn that trait from him while working there. The electronics store was already buzzing with the first few customers as she took her place behind the customer service desk to greet her first angry customer of the day.

"This robot vacuum is the stupidest thing I've ever bought! I want a refund."

"What's that smell?" replied Miriam.

The customer yelled back, "I was at work yesterday and my dog crapped on the floor and this stupid thing spent the rest of the day smearing it all over the carpet."

She knew she was supposed to smile politely and be helpful, but she couldn't hold back a nervous giggle. The idea of it all was a bit too funny. What did this guy think would happen? Miriam thought about how disappointing that experience would have been for her customer to come home to and considered her words carefully. She felt badly for him, and she smiled to put him at ease.

"I'm sorry sir, that sounds really terrible. Well, there's not much I can do about your carpet, and it sounds to me like the product performed exactly as it should but let me see what options I have available for you."

She took the machine to the repair center in the back and came out a few minutes later.

"Ok, so the vacuum was bought more than a month ago, which means that I can't give you the refund you requested. However, here's what I can do: my manager says I can sell you a new floor brush for 50% off, and I've asked the guys in the back to clean up the machine for you as best they can. They should be done in about an hour. If you can wait, go grab a coffee and maybe use the time to find a good carpet cleaner. When your vacuum is ready, I'll give you a call, and then I'll walk you through the setting on the app that controls the timing. My suggestion is that you have it run at night instead, when you and your dog are both asleep."

"I'm sorry I was sharp with you earlier," replied the customer, "I know it's not your fault… and I didn't know about the timer. Yeah, that would help a lot. I'll be back in an hour."

"It figures," thought Miriam… "Just a crazy start to another good day."

Your behaviors are the product of your attitude (thoughts and feelings), filtered through the lenses of your personality, experience, culture, religion, beliefs, and genetics, among other influences. However, regardless of the many layers of filters, your behavior goes through after they are determined by your attitude, they will inevitably take on the qualities of your default mindset, in categories I call *red mindset* and *green mindset*.

Green mindset

What do you think I mean when I say a green mindset? What does that look like? How do you feel? You can think of it as the foundation upon which your thoughts and feelings sit before they morph into attitudes, and eventually behaviors. In a green mindset, you'll find that you:

- Are able to deal with something that challenges you
- Are more courageous
- Feel little stress
- Are in a dominantly calm mood
- Have the ability to balance your thoughts and feelings regarding a situation you are dealing with
- Can think logically and rationally
- Can control any anger or frustration
- Can be in the present, in the now
- Are open to connecting to the people you interact with

In the green mindset, you are at your best, and when you are at your best you can deliver genuine and natural service to your customers. Do you think it has to all be positive to be in a green mindset?

We are human so there will always be things that challenge us, that doesn't mean you aren't in a green mindset. It is possible to be in a green mindset and still feel a little anxious, nervous, frustrated, and upset. But you can control your emotions, feelings, and thoughts and can put them into perspective for the situation.

Red mindset

What do you think I mean by a red mindset? What does that look like? How do you feel? In a red mindset, you'll find that you expend your energy:

- Just getting the job done (like a crap-covered robot)
- Looking out for your own interests
- Not being able to see the full picture
- Being inattentive
- Preoccupied with your own emotions, feelings, and thoughts
- Allowing your emotions, feelings, and thoughts to blow out of proportion
- Disconnected from people around you
- Feeling aggravated
- Unable to control irritation and frustration

In the red mindset, you are not the best you can be. It can range from a full-blown loss of control to something a little more subtle, like Miriam's casual dismissal of her customer's complaint. Either way, you will not be providing the best service you can to your customer.

Miriam's green mindset didn't prevent her from experiencing the customer's wrath, or the disgust associated with handling a machine full of crap. But she was able to find the humor in an otherwise terrible situation and remained open to empathizing with her customer in spite of him yelling at her. Her green mindset allowed her to see her customer's anger as something that was happening to him, not something that was happening to her. The customer wasn't angry with Miriam, but with the product, the company, and the situation.

Miriam's green mindset allowed her to search for options rather than an escape from the customer. Before that, she heard her boss's comment when she came in as a measure of his attentiveness and not how close to being late she was, and before that, she heard the song on the radio as a reminder that she should be grateful for the learning experience of a previous relationship, rather than a stab in the heart of a wounded lover.

A green mindset allows you to filter what happens in the world around you into an optimistic frame. Think about it, most of what happened in Miriam's external world was the same between her red and green mindset experiences. What changed wasn't the external triggers, but her internal experience of them.

It's important to note that we are all going to be pushed/moved into the red mindset from time to time, it is only natural and human. We aren't happy green mindset people all the time.

But why do we move into that red mindset? How does it happen?

And who do you think controls how you experience external triggers?

In customer service, your mindset and how you choose to react to triggers will make a difference to how well you handle situations and ultimately could be the difference between a customer receiving poor service or exceptional service. The difference between Miriam's bad day and Miriam's good day was her mindset, which steered her toward very different reactions to the same external triggers.

What is a trigger?

A trigger is something external that affects your emotional state and can affect your ability to be in the moment and be present in the situation that is happening.

What do you think a trigger could be?

- A thought
- A feeling
- Someone saying something to you
- The temperature in the room
- The time of day

- The feeling of being judged, criticized, teased, or put down
- Friction between co-workers
- Something not working
- A delay

Thinking of your own experiences – what has triggered you to move from a green to red mindset? These can be in your personal life or at work.

Can you think of a couple of examples of triggers that you have that send you instantly into a red mindset?

_____

_____

_____

Have you ever seen a driver on the road totally lose their minds with rage in their car? I saw a woman just the other day yelling and screaming, slamming her hands against the steering wheel... throwing a full-on temper tantrum while all alone in her vehicle.

I wondered what might have triggered her.

- Someone pulling in front of her
- Her kids in the back seat screaming

- She just had an argument on the phone with her husband and she hung up
- She is trying to get through a light that has just gone from amber to red

Who knows?????! These could all be triggers, and what triggers one person may not trigger someone else.

You have a choice about how you interpret a trigger. And you are responsible for allowing a trigger to move you into the red mindset. You can't blame what has happened or what someone has said or done to you, and you can't even blame the trigger. No one can make you feel anything, ever. Your feelings originate inside your head, and you can control them, you alone are responsible for them. Someone else's emotional response to a trigger might be totally different from yours.

No one wants to live in a world where someone outside of you can literally select your emotions for you on a phone on their app. How disempowering would that be if someone else could simply decide your mood? Yet, most of the time, many of us, are quick to blame other people or external triggers for how we feel, as though such an app actually exists.

You might not be proud of your choice, and you might not be intentional about it, but ultimately you choose to allow the trigger to either affect you and move you into the red mindset or ignore it or mitigate against it and stay in the green mindset.

How do you mitigate against it? By doing something to relieve or reduce how you feel. It could be to breathe, walk away, get someone else to help you, think nice thoughts. Whatever works for you to stop your emotions, feelings, thoughts to be blown out of proportion. Remember, the red mindset originates inside of your mind, so the green mindset can too.

What kinds of things help you to alleviate your triggers?

_____

_____

_____

_____

Do you know what used to really trigger me? When I was cabin crew, serving meals to passengers, one of them stood up and asked to use the bathroom while the food cart was in the aisleway. OMG, how annoying is that?! I really just wanted to tell them to sit down and let me do my job. But instead, I would smile and ask them to wait a minute while I closed up the cart and walked it all the way back to the galley so they could get past me to go to the bathroom. Internally I was at war with myself, red or green? Being that I could choose either mindset, which would I allow to win?

To choose your mindset, you need to be aware of what you're saying to yourself. You need to be aware of your inner voice.

Your inner voice

Here's the thing that makes choosing your mindset challenging. You're never really paying attention. You are probably thinking, "wait, what? I am not paying attention? But I am."

Nope. You're not. In fact, you're not really *paying attention* to what you're reading right now, because you're too distracted by the voice you're always listening to. You are always listening to yourself. You have that little voice in your head that's always saying something.

Your inner voice is probably picking a fight with me right now. It just told you that you are not *actually reading* this and probably something about how I'm wrong and you don't have a little voice in your head that's always talking to you.

Yep. That's the voice. The one that just told you it doesn't exist.

So, pay attention now. You can't turn off the voice in your head, but you can be aware of it. It'll say things like:

- *Should I say something?*
- *Should I stop reading and think about this for a bit?*

- *I'll just keep going and see what else is in this list of comments*
- *Wow she is still just writing stuff, just get to the point already*
- *Can I just skip to the next section?*
- *I better keep reading because I don't want to miss anything important*
- *Where is she going with this?*

We all have an inner voice that is talking to us <u>all the time</u>. It's making recommendations to try to help you adapt to the situation you're in and find your place in the world. But what if I told you that that little voice isn't actually you. It is just your self-talk, your inner speech, and it is basing its commentary on all the experiences you have had in the past. Decades of experience.

Whilst some self-talk is good and motivational, a lot of it can also be destructive. If you're not mindful of it, you can mistake the recommendations of your inner voice for imperative responses, and it can drive your feelings, actions, and eventually what comes out of your mouth, and your behavior.

Think about this, when you were a toddler, you didn't have a blueprint. If someone called you a bad name when you were four years old you wouldn't have known it was a bad name because you didn't have that experience yet. But as you got older and you gained experiences, you started to form that little inner voice. You started to have things to go off, to benchmark against to have an identity in, and all of a sudden life was never the same again.

Everything you do in the now, all of your thoughts, feelings, emotions, are all based on your past experiences. That is why my inner voice and your inner voice will be completely different from anyone else's inner voice.

Your inner voice is controlling you! And it's not even you. Do you know how I know it isn't you? Because you can negotiate with it, and you can decide not to listen to it. Do you think that is possible? Of course – you already do it now. It tells you something and then you do the opposite. It tells you not to eat the piece of cake, but you still do. Because the inner voice isn't you!

It tells you it doesn't even exist, but then you argue with it and tell it that it does exist, and the fact that you can argue with it means it's not you.

It's a cognitive recommender engine, like the "products you might also like" bar on a product page on Amazon. Based on your previous purchases, Amazon's recommender engine suggests things you should also consider. The inner voice does that for you in your mind. Based on your previous experiences, it's suggesting how you should interpret the experience you're in right now. You can take its advice, or not. Up to you.

NO ONE CAN MAKE YOU DO SOMETHING OR MAKE YOU FEEL A CERTAIN WAY. That is YOUR choice.

We all add meaning and significance to what other people do and say to us. That inner voice in your head, based on decades of experience, starts chat chat chatting! *He disrespected me, he was rude to me, she is picking on me, blah blah blah.*

There is always an ongoing conversation in your head with yourself, and this stops you from listening, considering other options, and it stops you from truly being present in the moment.

So, what can you do about it?

First, accept that it will always be there, and it will never go away. But by knowing it is there and by knowing you are driven by it, when you hear it, you can choose to detach yourself from it, consider other options, and perhaps chose not to listen to it. If you pay enough attention to it, you'll realize that its primary function is to help you feel included in the world and avoid feeling excluded.

It tells you who you should talk to, who you shouldn't, it tells you what to say and what not to say. It says, "well if you do that, *x* might happen."

Miriam's red mindset inner voice told her that the universe chose a song specifically to irritate her, that her boss's welcoming remark was a snide comment about her running late, and that her angry customer was yelling *at* her.

But none of those things were objectively true. Miriam's green mindset inner voice told her that the song was an opportunity for gratitude, her boss's comment was a learning opportunity, and her customer's comments were the voice of a frustrated man with a carpet full of crap at home, looking for someone to blame it on.

Your inner voice is just there, and it's not all-powerful.

So just let it be there, recognize that it is there, then choose not to listen to it and move on. It is only going to tell you whatever is already consistent with what you already know. If you've decided that today is a bad day, your inner voice will search for evidence to support what it already knows, but that impacts on your ability to be present in your current situation.

The loss of power you can experience in a situation all comes from the significance you put on the words and behaviors of what other people are saying and doing, and your inner voice's commentary on what those things might mean for you. It's as simple as that.

The more you are aware of all of this, the more you will be able to put aside the words and actions of others, and the running recommendations of your inner voice. When you recognize what is happening, you can choose behaviors that totally contradict what your inner voice is chattering on about.

What it is and what it means

Your inner voice very rarely talks to you about what's actually happening and almost always talks to you about what it means. But those are two very different things.

There are two main ingredients in your experience of all situations – WHAT IT IS and then WHAT IT MEANS – and this is true in every experience you have in life. In your memories of your past, it's what it was and what it meant.

The 'what it is' contains the facts, the real, actual words that were used, the true movements or activities of people or objects in the outside world. What actually happened. Whereas the 'what it means' is composed of the meaning you attach to the 'what it is,' and this is all based on all your past experiences as interpreted and related to you by your inner voice.

When something happens we automatically start to add meaning and significance to it. We can't help it. We start with the 'what it is' and then add the 'what it means' in order to build our experience of the world.

How you attach the 'what it means' to the 'what it is' will determine if you stay in the Green Mindset or are pushed into the Red Mindset. It's ultimately your choice. This is important in customer service because it objectively does not matter what another person is saying or doing. It only becomes significant when you attach significance to it by adding meaning.

So, it's up to you how you choose to let it affect you!

I recently had a crew member come to tell me, "One of my passengers said that I am a slave and I should do what he says, he disrespected me."

Now, let's take a look at this – what are the facts, what actually happened?

The passenger saying that the crew member is a slave is what happened. This is the 'what it is' because it is what actually happened; it is the truth, the passenger actually said those words. It is what it is.

From reading the crew member's comment, what do you think the crew member felt it meant?

The crew member felt disrespected, which is the 'what it means' to them. "Disrespected" is the meaning the crew member has chosen to attach to the 'what it is' (the actual event). And the 'what it means' he/she created from the 'what it is' is based on all of the crew member's past experiences. Another crew member in the exact same scenario might create a completely different 'what it means'.

Being called a slave is what happened and feeling disrespected is what it meant (to that particular crew member at that particular time).

In Miriam's red mindset, the customer yelled *at her*. But in her green mindset, the customer yelled *because he was upset*. Same 'what it is' and totally different 'what it means', and the difference didn't occur in the environment around Miriam, it occurred in her mind. It was a mindset choice.

If red mindset Miriam was aware of her inner voice, she might have questioned the recommendation that she interprets the customer's yelling as being directed *at her* personally. She might have considered the possibility that what the customer was expressing had nothing to do with Miriam at all. And then she might have been able to shift into a green mindset and change both what it meant to her, and her experience of the event.

What meaning will you create for yourself in your experience of the world, and of your work in customer service? What meaning will you find in the relationships you have with your customers, colleagues, and manager? If you have a green mindset, and you are aware of your inner voice, do you think you will have an easier time building a good experience for yourself and those around you? Would you see yourself as a stronger member of a stronger team?

6

TEAMING

I worked at Emirates Airlines as cabin crew for more than a decade before moving to IntrepidAir. I absolutely loved it. I would fly to London, Paris, Melbourne, or any number of destinations, each time with a crew that I had only met that day. With tens of thousands of cabin crew on the roster, I could fly for months or years without flying two flights with the same person, and on those rare occasions when I flew with another crew member that I had flown with before, it was a pleasant surprise, and I would take the time to get to know them better.

Most of the time though, as a Purser on a large aircraft, I would have a team of up to two dozen crew onboard that I had only met in the briefing room minutes before boarding the flight with them. Even though each of us was properly dressed and groomed in our highly tailored and precisely homogenous uniforms, we were strangers to each other.

Now I want you to think about that for a minute. Think about every flight you've been on, from anywhere to anywhere. The crew all know what to do. They have particular roles to play. They know when to stand where, how to act, and what to say. When the service carts are moving steadily down the aisle, and you see the crew handing things to each other, coordinating perfectly, grabbing things for each other from the galley, finishing off each other's drink order for the passengers, and moving together as in a fast-paced but elegant game of rapid-fire mile-high restaurant service… make a note that it is most likely that all of those crew were strangers to each other that morning, as much so as they were to you.

Notice it next time. Think about it. And ask yourself: how do they do it? How do they move like that? Almost always predicting each other's needs. Nearly always with a smile and the occasional laugh. In those unfortunate moments when things might get tense due to a passenger's unmet expectations, how do they back each other up, take over for each other, hand off conversations to each other so smoothly, and fulfill promises made to passengers on each other's behalf? How can strangers behave like that?

It's actually a very learnable set of skills called teaming, a term originally coined by Amy Edmondson.[8]

The difference between teaming and teamwork is that teaming is done "on the fly" (pun totally intended). Teamwork involves people who stay together for a while and learn how to work together, as well as their roles, individual personalities, stress behaviors, and capabilities, working on how to maximize shared strengths and mitigate known weaknesses. On the other hand, teaming is more like a pick-up game, with people thrown together into a team project (for example, a flight) without any time to practice together. Roles shift rapidly, there is the potential for cultural clashes, and there is little or no time to get to know one another. In other words, teaming is the formation of a team, not its smooth operation.

Think about an all-star basketball team. The players in the game are all coming from different teams. They don't know each other well, and they're even likely to have played against each other at times. Suddenly they are thrown together onto the court to play alongside each other, and with little to no practice time together. They don't really know each other's strengths and weaknesses, and yet they are expected to perform well together on a fast-formed team of relative strangers. The process of these

8   Edmondson, Amy C. Teaming: How Organizations Learn, Innovate, and Compete in the Knowledge Economy. Jossey-Bass, 2012.

strangers learning rapidly to behave well as a team is the process of teaming.

This also happens in large hospitals, where emergency room team members are changing all the time. Each shift, the emergency room team can change. A surgical team that works together once, might never again perform surgery again as that particular team. It's vital in the emergency room and the operating theatre that the team members learn quickly how to work well together, even if they will only be together for that one shift or a particular surgery. Lives are literally at stake if they don't communicate well.

In the airline industry, your team is almost always new. Often your team is disbanded at the end of the flight before you even have had a chance to gel. With traditional teamwork, a team has time to go through the stages of team development known as Forming – Storming – Norming – and Performing.[9] However, with a cabin crew team, you don't get to go through these phases, you don't have time. At IntrepidAir they get together for a short briefing and are then shipped out on a bus to an aircraft where they have a list of jobs that need to be done in a very short time, and then suddenly passengers begin boarding the aircraft. There is no time to go through the traditional team development stages. There's no norming! Ever!

---

9   Tuckman, Bruce W (1965). "Developmental sequence in small groups". Psychological Bulletin. 63 (6): 384–399.

What makes it possible for cabin crew to know exactly what needs to be done and when and by who?

It's the rules, the procedures, and the training that makes it possible. They can get onboard a flight and they may never have worked with any of the people in their team before, but they all know exactly what needs to be done, when it needs to be done, how long they have to do it, and who is responsible for what. It's a bit like a jazz band. Although each musician is autonomous and plays their own instrument and music, they listen to each other and play together. That's how great jazz music is played, without practice. That's how teaming works.

Do you know how many employees Google has? Well over 100,000. And how many teams do they have? Thousands. The majority of Google's teams are teams that are set up for short projects, sometimes across different countries. A few years ago, Google set out on a quest to figure out what makes a team successful. After interviewing hundreds of employees and teams they found five things that affect team effectiveness.[10] Each of them can be executed in any service or project team in any company. I'll paraphrase and expand on each of the five principles.

---

10   Rozovsky, J. 2015. The five keys to a successful Google team. Retrieved from: https://rework.withgoogle.com/blog/five-keys-to-a-successful-google-team/

Trust

In order for a team to succeed, it's essential for members to trust each other. This gives them the confidence to take risks and be exposed in front of one another. In addition to trusting their teammates to take risks, they also need to trust that they will not be punished if they themselves make a mistake.

There are a lot of ways for leaders to build trust. For example:

- Use people's names: People love hearing their own names. Why? This is the name your mother called you, the first set of sounds you heard that you knew referred only to you. Before you meet your team, know their names so you can address them directly.
- Eye contact: How much is too much? Nine seconds. Between two to five seconds is the appropriate amount. Less than two seconds indicates you are trying to avoid them. More than nine seconds and the other person will likely transition into the flight, fight, or flirting mode.
- Open posture: Having an open posture communicates vulnerability, and that you don't expect any threats, it builds trust. Keep your hands visible, and your arms and legs uncrossed.
- Ask for input, ideas, and opinions: During your first meeting or in challenging situations, a leader might say, "I want to hear from you, I may miss something." Leaders should acknowledge that they themselves are capable of making

mistakes or forgetting to do something. We are all human and everyone knows it. Acknowledging that creates more trust.

- Reinforce helpful behaviors with positive feedback: Tell them if they've done a good job. Everyone loves a bit of encouragement and recognition for doing well.

- Develop your team: Coach someone that isn't as experienced as you are. Rather than giving out answers, ask for solution ideas and see what happens. People will learn more, faster if they discover the solutions on their own.

- Delegate to your team: You can express trust in your team by giving them opportunities. The challenge is that those opportunities often come with risk. You might need to manage the outcome if a team member makes a mistake.

- Encourage open communication: Transparency and trust go hand in hand. Open communication will only come when you extend trust and your team trusts you in return.

- Demonstrate that you have trust in your team: If your team member comes to you with a problem, try telling them that you trust them to work it out and just to let you know what they did. Give them the space to work it out and if they fail then tell them not to worry, everything is fixable. Also, remember not all teams are the same, what happened before, may not happen again.

- Demonstrate engagement: Be present and focused in conversation, show you are listening. A good leader should be listening about 70% of the time during a conversation and talking about 30% of the time.

Now, take a moment and identify three things that you can do in order to increase the level of trust in your team. Focus on behaviors and actions rather than ideas and attitudes.

1. _____

2. _____

3. _____

Dependability

This is when team members get things done on time. On a flight, it means arriving at the briefing on time, securing the cabin on time, checking the toilets on time, etc. Dependability also includes credibility... when you say you will do something you follow through with it. For example, if you say that you will bring a blanket to a passenger, you bring the blanket to the passenger so that the passenger doesn't get irritated and take out their frustration on one of your teammates.

In an airline, crew members can exhibit dependability by making sure that the tasks associated with their roles are done on time. Crew members can be role models in this. They can be on time for briefing, show up prepared, and complete all their paperwork. They can be consistent and exhibit what they expect from others. In terms of grooming and uniform, for example, there's no point in providing feedback on the quality of another team member's uniform when you yourself have a crease in yours.

And most importantly: DWYSYWD – do what you say you will do. This is one of the most important leadership traits. The acronym was coined in Kousez and Pozner's *The Leadership Challenge*. In their study of 75,000 leaders worldwide, they found that the most important quality of a leader is credit-ability and that the most missing quality in leadership is also credibility.[11] DWYSYWD is their way of making it easy to remember that credibility comes from the matching of words and behavior. Remember people judge us by what we do and say, not by our intentions.

Be honest with yourself now. In what ways have you given your-self credit for your intentions, but haven't backed them up with what you do and say? Try to note down three ways in which you would like to become more dependable and build credibility with your team:

1. _____

2. _____

3. _____

---

[11]   Kouzes, J. M., & Posner, B. Z. (2017). The leadership challenge (6th ed.). John Wiley & Sons.

Structure and clarity

The third main ingredient in effective teaming is a clear structure and communications. This includes a number of smaller ingredients, such as clear roles and assigned positions, plans, and goals. These might also include Standard Operating Procedures (SOPs), or safety and service procedures. It's important in teaming to regularly communicate team goals, not just when the team meets for the first time, but throughout the teaming exercise. It's important that the team is constantly communicating about what is coming next in order to ensure shared expectations and effective decision-making processes.

Have you ever been to a restaurant with an open kitchen, one that can be seen from the seating area? Did you notice how much communication is going on back there? A kitchen team needs to balance the timing of dishes and service perfectly to make sure a table's entire order is ready at the same time. The meats, vegetables, and sauces all take different preparation times, and the kitchen may be dealing with dozens of dishes all at once. That requires clear structured preparation procedures, and clear consistent coordination between the kitchen staff to ensure accuracy and quality in service delivery. The waiter can only deliver to the customer what the kitchen prepares.

Leaders investing in teaming in any service industry should have a constant clarity dialogue going with their team members. They should make an effort to explain the reasons behind decisions, especially if there is any deviation from the normal processes or procedures. They should try to include the team in decisions whenever possible, allowing them to contribute and facilitate the answers to challenges.

Regular communication with the team helps them to know what is expected. No one can read your mind, and leaders can't deliver all their expectations in an initial meeting. Think about it in terms of a flight crew during a twelve-hour day, if the senior cabin crew member lists all their expectations in the briefing, the team won't remember everything. Instead, the senior should feed their expectations to their team throughout the shift. For example, ten minutes before the top of decent, a senior might tell their crew that they would like everyone to start preparing the cabin as soon as they hear the high/low chime, as the passengers may be sleeping and if it's a full flight it will take longer than normal to secure the cabin. They may also add pre-emptive clarification, such as, "but be careful not to insist people fasten their seatbelts if they don't want to, remember the seatbelt sign does not come on until later."

In a restaurant kitchen, it's good practice for the chef to have a team briefing before each day's service. A good chef will prepare their team for work by clarifying expectations, revisiting challenges and opportunities from the previous day, and providing tips on the preparation that can save time and prevent mistakes. Throughout the duty, a good chef is in constant communication with their team, coordinating the timing of dishes, ensuring the quality of the ingredients, and listening to teammates who might be overwhelmed and in need of their support.

In what ways can you improve by adding clarity and structure to your team's service activities? People can't be expected to fulfill unspoken expectations, so try to list three expectations that you would like to see fulfilled on your team that you can share with them:

1. _____

2. _____

3. _____

Meaning

Teaming is most effective when the work is personally important to the team members, the work that they do for the team is meaningful to them as individuals. This, by the way, is the subject of this book: finding meaning in customer service. What Google discovered is that those teams whose members find their work meaningful, gel together better and faster, and perform better. They are naturally better at teaming.

Leaders can help by reminding their team that what they are doing is meaningful, and by modeling the meaningfulness of the team's tasks. By pointing out to the team how what they do is meaningful and what they do and say makes a difference to themselves, their team, and their customers.

On a flight, cabin crew can highlight impact by giving recognition to other crew members for their actions and words and linking those behaviors to an impact. For example, "I saw the way you approached that passenger when he came to the galley. You were really approachable and friendly. That is the type of behavior that makes our passengers want to fly with us again and that means our company does well."

Or perhaps, "I saw the way you all worked together to get the service done a lot quicker than most. Fantastic job and I'm proud to have had you as my team today. Being organized and proactive and getting the service done faster meant our passengers got their rubbish collected quicker and they could rest sooner. It is the small things like that that make our passengers come to fly with us again, and that means our company does well."

A butcher in their shop can add meaning to work by reminding their staff that the meat they are preparing is destined for someone's family table. It's perhaps the centerpiece of a celebration, or the fuel required to turn a young boy into a star athlete. The preparation of good quality food for families not only ensures the growth and success of the families that they are serving, but in exchange also ensures the growth and success of the families of the butcher's employees.

The head mechanic at an auto repair shop can remind their team that each car sitting in their shop represents a family or business that is under stress due to the temporary loss of transportation. Children need to get to school, and parents need to get to work. Packages are waiting to be delivered, and homes are waiting to be shifted. The customers to whom those vehicles belong are in a state of anxiety, managing the absence of a very important tool for their effectiveness, and hoping for a fast and complete return of their vehicle. Not only are the families and businesses who own those vehicles counting on support from their mechanics to return their chaos into order, but the families of the mechanics too will be cared for by a steady stream of income from satisfied customers.

Also, remember that the work you are doing in customer service is meaningful to you because it's leading you toward the achievement of your personal goals. You're not an idiot, so if there was a better way for you to achieve your personal goals, you'd probably be doing that instead. You might not enjoy every aspect of your work, but you can find meaning in the value that that work brings to you and your family in terms of finances, or to your career in terms of training and experience. You have a vision for your life, and the work you are doing now is a major piece of your journey toward that vision right now.

Your goals might include better education options for your kids, a new home, healthcare for your aging parents, or your next vacation to a dream destination. You might be aiming for a specific job in the future of your career, and the experience you are gaining now is in preparation for that job. Or you might be working to build value into the lives of those that are working with you: your colleagues, students, leaders, or teammates.

In what ways is your current customer service role contributing to your personal vision for your personal life, career, and goals?

1. _____

2. _____

3. _____

Impact

Team members value knowing that their work matters to others as well, not only to them. Team members like to understand how the team's efforts contribute to organizational or broader social goals. It may be that the work of the team is enabling the whole organization to reach a goal, or that the team's work is contributing to a larger corporate social responsibility target.

On the individual level, customer service by its very definition has an impact on every single customer that experiences it. That's a human life, impacted.

For example, a senior cabin crew member might say to their team of cabin crew, "I know for us this is just another flight but for some of our passengers today they have probably saved all year in order to afford the flight to see their family, others it might have been two years or more. They have invited you to be a part of their meaningful experience. Make it one they won't forget."

Or perhaps, "None of our passengers are on the flight today because they were sat at home bored, they are on our flight for a reason. We have the power to create more meaning for them just through the little things that we do and say today."

You might be thinking that your service role is less meaningful for your customers because it's a simpler role, or perhaps detached from direct customer interactions. For instance, imagine a mechanic in an auto repair shop. The mechanic isn't in direct communication with the customer most of the time, but the service is provided for the customer directly anyway as they are working on the customer's vehicle.

But when was the last time your car broke down conveniently? Or when have you ever brought your car in for service because you were bored? Never, right? Each vehicle in that shop belongs to a family that needs it to drive kids to school, get to work, or bring food home. Or a vehicle in the shop may belong to a company whose clients are not getting their supplies on time, and the company is suffering a lack of productivity because the vehicle is broken down or in need of service. Those vehicles in the repair shop are no less meaningful to their owners than an airline flight is to its passengers.

Every guest seated at your restaurant has a reason for having chosen your restaurant. Every guest in your hotel has a purpose behind their visit. Every passenger on your bus. Every customer that buys groceries from your store. Everyone wandering into your store to look for a new shirt. Every person seated in your theatre. Every patient in your clinic. All of them... they have all come for a kind of service, and in doing so, they have invited you into a brief moment where your life intersects with theirs. They are all counting on your service to make that experience meaningful.

Leaders can also model other behaviors that show that they think what the team is doing is meaningful. Some behaviors include speaking highly of other people, being enthusiastic, being involved, being motivated, talking positively about the company, etc.

Why is what you are doing in customer service meaningful to your customers?

1. _____

2. _____

3. _____

What are their expectations of a meaningful service experience from you?

1. _____

2. _____

3. _____

Now I'd like to invite you to consider the impact of the answers you've recorded to the questions posed in the five teaming conditions above and determine how you as a customer service agent can bring these to the team you are working with now. How will you invest in building trust? What are some ways you can be dependable and communicate credibility? How can you contribute to role and task clarity? What meaning can you find for yourself in your work? What impact will your work have on others? If you achieve even half of what you've written down above, how might that transform the performance of your team, and your experience of work?

7

EMPOWERMENT

Each day members of my cabin crew wake up on their own. They shower, get dressed, brush their teeth. They choose what to wear and what to eat for breakfast. They will check their schedules, reply to messages, and arrange transportation for themselves. They put fuel in their gas tanks and pay for their taxis. In fact, they manage all their finances on their own. They pay their bills, save up for big purchases, plan vacations, and apply for loans. They know how to manage themselves in a complex society made up of thousands of laws, cultural norms, and social expectations that they need to navigate every day in order to participate well as citizens and residents of Dubai.

I have incredible volumes of adulting capacity in my team. So why should I expect them to be any less capable at work? The rules at work are fewer than in the wider society that they live in. The number of things they need to manage is fewer too, and less complex than the things they take care of in their regular lives. The kinds of relationships at work are less complex too, there are clear lines of responsibility and authority... not like in their families, neighborhoods, or social groups where less clarity can lead to unintended confusion or offenses. The resources at work are simpler than those they manage in their everyday lives too. At work, the resources come with clear instructions. Life is more defined at work, and therefore, simpler.

They live quite happily and function all on their own in society, and for some strange reason tend to need a manager once they get to work. Why is that?

Why do we even need managers? The people that are in your team all know how to do their jobs. Just like they all know how to get up in the morning, look after kids, manage finances, drive cars without getting into accidents, make decisions about what they are going to eat – all without a boss. They make hundreds of decisions every day without a boss. So why is it they need to be told what to do at work?

If your team needs to be managed in order to do things that they have been trained to do, are capable of doing, and can be expected to do as functioning adults, they are being micromanaged. And your team will remain perpetually imma-ture *because* they are being micromanaged.

I have an eight-year-old son who eats all on his own. I don't have to spoon-feed him like I did when he was a baby. Why? Because he's of a reasonable age and experience level to be able to handle feeding himself. In fact, he would be seriously irritated at me now if I started to spoon-feed him again. He would likely rebel. I can imagine the look on his face crossing from confusion to disgust as he physically takes the spoon out of my hand saying, "Stop that, mummy, I can feed myself. You're micromanaging me, you're being ridiculous."

This simple principle is too often overlooked when adults come into the workforce. Each and every skill they develop will only be developed when the person who first fed them, stops feeding them. And for that, the person who teaches them to eat must also be willing to clean up the mess they make as they learn to do it on their own. The unwillingness of managers to clean up the mess while their team members are learning to be autono-mous is the number one contributing factor in micromanage-ment. The antidote to all this ineffectiveness is empowerment.

Empowerment is when authority and accountability are del-egated. Team members are free to feed themselves and make a mess in the process of learning, knowing that the manager will help clean it up if required. Proper empowerment results in bet-ter motivation, inspiration, and engagement. This in turn:

1. Increases job satisfaction: when your team knows you and when you trust them and have their backs, they'll do their best.
2. Solves problems faster: because you trust your team to make a decision, customers don't have to wait for you to come and speak to them.
3. Improves customer service: because your team has the freedom to do whatever it takes to satisfy a customer (obviously within reason).

Be the kind of person who empowers your team to make decisions and act independently. Think of it as a more adulty form of adulting. So, there are two relationships we want to explore here. The first relationship is how you can empower your team, and the second is how your company can empower you.

Just like a child learning to eat, the first few times any adult does anything, they'll probably make some mistakes. But that's how humans of all ages learn things: we try, make mistakes, and hopefully, we have someone better than us coaching us through them and protecting us from the consequences of those mistakes. On your team, it should be okay and safe to fail, but just as your team expects you to protect them from their mistakes, they should also be expected to learn from them. If the same mistakes keep happening, then you will need to talk through that with them and see how you can best help them move forward.

I would be seriously concerned if my son still dropped more food on the floor than he got into his mouth at dinner.

Empowerment is made up of delegated authority and account-ability. Getting things done starts with an approving authority (that's YOU) passing authority and accountability on to another person. Or when your manager passes authority and account-ability to you.

And on that note, don't be afraid to wrestle the spoon away from your manager. Nobody likes a helicopter manager any more than a helicopter parent.

Imagine for a moment a relay race at the Olympics. Runners circle the track carrying a baton. As they run, they pass the baton on to the next runner. What's the safest way to ensure a good pass of the baton? Well, a runner should come to a com-plete stop, pass the baton with both hands to the next runner, and then the next runner should start running. However, this method is too slow to win. Instead, relay runners find them-selves in a much less safe and more complex game in order to move quickly. If the baton is passed on even a second too early or reached for just a second too late, it will fall. By not passing the baton quickly enough, the team will lose speed and will lose time. They need to get the hand-off just right.[12]

Empowerment is the baton handoff of authority and account-ability between you and your team. If you try to pass it before

12   Bradt, George. 2016. Accountability: The Essential Link Between Empowerment And Engagement. Forbes. Retrieved from https://www.forbes.com/sites/georgebradt/2016/02/16/accountability-the-essential-link-between-empowerment-and-engagement/?sh=3042b4562a4a

the team member is ready, willing, and able, and they can't manage it, you'll drop it. Pass it too late, with too much overlap, and the team member will feel micromanaged, and they will feel like you don't trust them. Waiting for you to hand off the baton is disempowering, and leads to disengagement, and other operating inefficiencies.

Once accountability and authority have been passed, you must get out of the way. You still have the right to approve or decline certain decisions, and a good manager remains available to provide advice and direction as needed, but you have to give your team members room to make decisions.

When your team member comes to you for management, don't automatically tell them what to do. Ask them what they would do. Coach and empower your team to make decisions. You should be available to guide them if needed. Be the kind of person who empowers people in your team. Be more willing to pick up the fallen baton from time to time than you are willing to hold on to it for too long.

Just as empowerment is accountability and authority, accountability is made up of feedback and consequence. The team member must understand that whilst you are empowering them, that doesn't mean that they can make any decision they like and never experience consequences for their choices. There are still consequences should a decision be made that isn't quite right.

I know you are faced with lots of different situations and issues throughout your workday, with different members of your team. Sometimes it will be difficult to spend time with each team member explaining all of this. And if you are a team member with a micromanager that won't let go of the baton, what can you do? You need to tell your manager. They might not recognize it, but nothing will change if you don't say anything.

In your next team meeting. Be the kind of person who makes your team or manager feel trusted, that makes them feel like you believe in them and that they can and should believe in you.

As a manager/leader yourself, you might choose a few empowering statements to get this message across, such as:

"We all know the same processes and procedures and I trust you to make decisions."

"Remember if you make a decision that deviates from the policy, you need to inform me so I am aware of it."

"I expect you to take ownership of decisions you make, and I am here should you need help or advice."

"You won't be punished for making mistakes if you are genuinely trying to achieve customer satisfaction. I've got your back."

Remember what you are doing will also encourage others to do the same. You need to choose to be the kind of person who:

- Makes your team feel trusted
- Makes them feel you believe in them
- Has open communication
- Creates an environment where they will come to you
- Listens to them
- Forgives mistakes!

As a member of my team, you can make as many mistakes as you want to in order to learn the job. But you can't hide them and you can't repeat them. Those are the only kinds of mistakes that I can't support you in.

Remember that trust is earned. You may not have their trust if you are changing your past micromanagement patterns to new empowerment patterns, but you can earn it. Your team may take time to trust the new you. This will probably be measured in months, not days.

I encourage you to now write down three things you will personally do to empower your team. Then beside each of the three things, I want you to identify the actions you will need to take to achieve them.

How will you empower your team?	What actions are needed from you to accomplish this?

Remember you'll need to be the kind of person who makes this happen. Your ideas are only intentions at the moment, so they won't mean anything to your team unless you make them happen. Just as a suggestion, why not ask your manager to hold you accountable to ensure your ideas are turned into actions? It would be a good way for you to introduce the topic to your manager and invite some feedback on your new empowerment strategy.

Let's recap – what is the result of a more empowered team?

- More engagement
- Motivation
- Team members are more inspired
- Problems are solved faster
- Improved customer service
- Allows for development
- Makes someone more willing and able to be involved and positively contribute

Everything that I have covered here applies to you personally. I want you to feel empowered to make the decisions to ensure that you are safe, your team is motivated, encouraged, and empowered, and that you exceed the expectations of your customers' needs. I want you to do what you need to do, to make sure your customers are experiencing your service in a way that results in long-lasting memories that they will share with others for years to come.

In case you find yourself in an organization that holds itself back by punishing its people for honest mistakes, now might be a good time to consider leaving a copy of this book on your manager's desk.

8

TURNING IT AROUND

I received this message on WhatsApp from one of my cabin crew not so long ago, and I think it might help you to see it before we continue.

> Hello everyone. Wanted to share this extra mile we had on board a flight yesterday.
>
> We had a passenger who was unsatisfied with Wi-Fi, which worked for 10 minutes after take-off and then was off the whole flight. While addressing his complaint, we asked how we could make his day better, and got to know that we had two new married couples on board going on their honeymoons. The dissatisfied customer asked us if

instead of doing something for him, we might do something special for the two newlywed couples.

We decided to give them a special moment in the sky and offered each of them a glass of champagne with sweets and a chocolate bar, along with crew greetings. The captain joined in the fun and did a welcome announcement for them as well. The passengers were surprised and happy, and they all asked to have pictures with the crew.

The gentleman without WIFI ended up feeling connected just the same, but it was just a different kind of connection than the one he had originally asked for.

In your role, you might frequently have to deal with customers who have complaints or are not happy with the product or the service. When dealing with that kind of situation it is important to remember that every situation is different, and you need to consider the current context and not necessarily rely on what worked or didn't work in the past.

It happens from time to time that a passenger onboard one of our flights needs a vegetarian meal, and we have none left. Can you imagine the passenger's disappointment? One time our staff might offer for them to buy snacks from the buy-on-board cart. The passenger might be happy with that solution. But on the next flight, the exact same thing could happen, and our crew could offer the same solution only to find the passenger starts yelling at them, blaming the crew for running out of vegetarian meals, and asking to speak to the senior crew member on board. There's no silver bullet solution. All issues, all solutions, and all mistakes are all contextual. There's no consistently perfect answer in customer service because each customer brings their own personality, culture, biases, values, history, and mood to the experience with you.

I want you to be the kind of person who feels empowered to make decisions to turn a service failure into a customer delight. I want you to try and avoid your customers going home and then writing to your company to complain about you or your team, or even worse, putting their complaints on social media or a review website. You have the power to turn a customer service experience around in the simple things you say or do, even if you can't fix the problem.

When things don't go by the book, don't be afraid to step away from the book. You might need to make a decision to deviate from the procedure because something has changed in your normal day. The procedures are there to cover 99% of your service experience, but sometimes you might need to not be so black and white. In aviation, when making a decision, you have to balance safety, operation, and customer service. What do you have to balance in your industry? You have to consider the benefits and costs of all options available to you in the moment.

These are the steps I teach my crew at IntrepidAir: LEOBER

Step 1: L – Listen to the customer and/or the team member.

Step 2: E – Empathize: make sure you understand what the problem or issue is. Put yourself in their shoes.

Step 3: O – Options: identify what options are available

Step 4: B – Brief: inform the customer/team member of the options available and let them decide

Step 5: E – Execute the chosen option

Step 6: R – Review: monitor the situation and follow-up with the customer

Let's look at each of these in detail.

Step 1: LISTEN

Most people most of the time are okay with things not going their way, as long as they feel listened to, understood and valued. This is true of most customers as well. So, the foundation of a good turn-around is active listening.

- Let the customer speak
- Do not interrupt them
- Hold off trying to solve the problem in your head
- Avoid judgment

At this point, you should be listening to what they are saying, and you can't do that if you have already started considering your options in your head. If you do, you may miss vital information. Focus on listening and understanding, *not* on solving the problem. Your job now is to listen and not make judgments on what the person is saying, how they are saying it, the tone of their voice, or the volume of their voice.

Step 2: EMPATHIZE

During this part of the process, you should still have your mouth closed 90% of the time, and only open it to ask clarifying questions or to repeat back what you have heard to show that you understand and empathize with the customer's experience. Remember, whether they are "right" or "wrong" isn't important right now. What matters is that they are having an experience, and they have invited you to help curate that experience with them.

- Ask questions to get more information
- Ask questions to further clarify information they have already given you
- Paraphrase what you have heard and repeat it back to them
- Identify what the actual problem is

People will feel heard and understood by you when you can summarize the information they have given you. For example,

"So what I am hearing from you is that when you were getting off the bus to board the aircraft, a man approached you and took your bag but didn't give you a tag for it?" The solutions will come, but not until the problem is fully understood.

Step 3: OPTIONS

Now you have to consider the options that are available to you by considering the available resources at your disposal. What do you have around you in terms of product, service, people, talent, time, and policy that you can use to alleviate the customer's concern? Once you have determined the options, you will then need to evaluate them – is there justification, and is the cost acceptable? And we are going to look at these two in detail.

JUSTIFICATION

Your decisions must be justified to fit the situation you are facing. Justification is the process of proving something is right or reasonable or proving that there is a good reason to do something.

For example, upgrading a passenger to business class because he didn't get a window seat in economy is not justified. That's a major upgrade for a small inconvenience, and we would go broke if everyone that wanted a window seat was upgraded to business class for free.

In a restaurant, you shouldn't give out free meals just because your customer doesn't like the taste. If there was no mistake from the kitchen, then the customer received what the customer ordered. Giving out complimentary meals due to the customer's error in judgment is not good for business.

You also can't just make up your own processes and procedures or do things your own way. That's not a justification, and bear in mind that if you develop a pattern of making decisions that are not justified, your supervisors will likely want to address that more deeply.

Here are a couple of examples of justifications that I've received:

A lady in economy approached me and begged for a pillow. According to her, she had terrible back pain. She explained she had a slipped disc. It was explained to her that such requests normally are not allowed as pillows are not provided in economy. However, for her condition, I explained we can make an exception and I provided her with the pillow discreetly. I also informed her that she can get this complimentary on her next flight if she books business class or pre orders a pillow through our duty free on our website. I checked on her during the flight and at the end of the flight was very thankful for the help we offered.

A passenger boarded with a broken leg however his seat choice prevented him from extending his leg due to the cast. I tried to find a row of three seats in economy, but due to the flight being nearly full, it was not possible. The last two rows in business class were vacant so I decided to move him to one of those seats so his leg could be straight and it would have support. This was the only way we could accept him for travel on the flight today and I didn't want to offload him as I know the next flight isn't for two days.

What do you think? Were these actions justified?

Can you think of a time when a customer service experience was falling apart and you had to do something outside of the normal policy in order to turn the experience around? Write it here:

_____

_____

_____

Was the action you took justified? How do you know?

COST

You also have to consider the cost of your decisions, and I don't just mean monetary cost here, either. It isn't just the cash value that the option is going to cost the company that needs to be considered, but also the cost of your time or someone's else's time, the cost to the perception of the customer or other customers, the cost of possibly disempowering someone with an option, and the cost of losing a customer, or worse, the cost of turning a customer into an anti-ambassador for your company.

This is how I have taught my crew members to evaluate cost at IntrepidAir. The chart has two axis – on the vertical side we have the Benefits/Customer Satisfaction/Likelihood of Resolving an Issue, and on the horizontal side, we have Costs. When looking at an option to solve an issue with a customer you will need to quickly think through – what are the benefits and what are the costs, and mentally plot it on the graph. This will help you identify if an option is acceptable, acceptable but with a cost, or not acceptable.

For example, let's say you are looking at the options for solving that passenger issue I mentioned earlier – someone complaining that he didn't get a vegetarian meal.

What options might be available to you?

1. Give him nothing and apologize (it is still an option!)
2. Give him a crew vegetarian hot meal
3. Give him a complimentary buy-on-board vegetarian hot option
4. Give him a vegetarian business class hot meal if there is one that hasn't been taken
5. Plate up some vegetarian salad and cheese from business class
6. Offer him a complimentary noodle cup from the buy-on-board cart

As I go through these options, put yourself in the shoes of a crew member onboard one of our flights, considering all the resources available to them 36,000 feet above the earth, with hundreds of pages of policies and procedures in their heads and a disappointed and hungry passenger in front of them.

Option 1 – Give him nothing and apologize – this will most likely result in low satisfaction as the passenger gets nothing, and likely to result in a high cost as the passenger may not return to us. Plus, he is likely to tell his family and friends about the bad experience, and then they may also not fly with us. Remember, people will tell at least fifteen others about a bad customer service experience.

Option 2 – Give him a crew vegetarian meal – these are for the cabin crew but come from the same supplier as for the passengers – this would likely result in high satisfaction as the passenger is still getting a hot meal and would be low cost to the company as the meal would be disposed of anyway at the end of the flight. This would only be an option if there wasn't a crew member needing the meal for themselves.

Option 3 – Give him a complimentary buy-on-board vegetarian hot option (wraps, pizzas, etc.) – this would likely result in medium/high satisfaction as he is getting something hot, although it is not a meal. And this option would incur low/medium cost to the company as it will be disposed of at the end of the flight if left unsold anyway. The risk is that the item might have been sold and the cost captured as income rather than a loss.

Option 4 – Give him a vegetarian business class meal that is unserved – this would likely result in high satisfaction as the passenger is getting a hot meal (of a higher standard than expected) and at low cost to the company (since it would have been disposed of anyway at the end of the flight if left uneaten).

Option 5 – Plate up some vegetarian salad and cheese from business class unused meals and crew meals – this would likely result in medium satisfaction as it isn't a hot meal, but at least the passenger is getting something to eat. And this would be a low cost to the company as the food offered would have been disposed of at the end of the flight anyway.

Option 6 – Offer him a complimentary noodle cup – this would likely result in low satisfaction as it is not a hot meal or fresh food and would be a high cost to the company as it is a saleable item that would not otherwise be disposed of (unless this is the only option because the other options are not available).

Plotting these options on the chart above, we have narrowed it down to three acceptable choices – 2, 4, and 5. And always remember a combination of options might be the best option.

Step 4: BRIEF

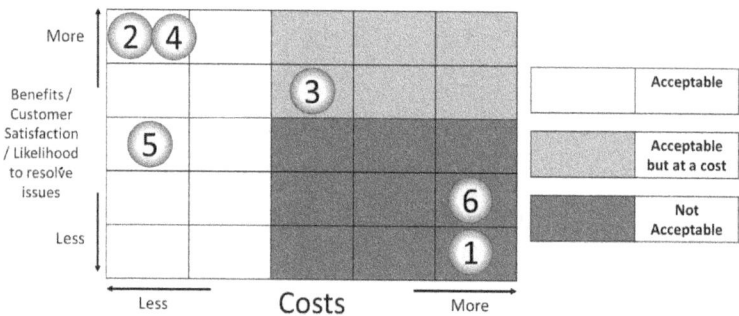

So, we have our three acceptable choices – 2, 4, and 5:

Option 2 – Give him a crew vegetarian hot meal
Option 4 – Give him a vegetarian business class hot meal that is left over
Option 5 – Plate up some vegetarian salad and cheese from business class leftover meals and crew meals

Which one would you choose in this situation?

That was a trick question. It doesn't matter what you would choose. It's not your experience we are trying to turn around here.

The next step is to brief the customer on their options and to ask them what they want. Most people, most of the time, don't mind making compromises on their expectations as long as they are empowered to choose the alternative.

In our example, you couldn't possibly know what the passenger will want, even if you've dealt with this situation before. Every customer is unique. One passenger may want a hot meal but another may hate airline hot meals and would love some salad and cheese. If you have more than one option, you should always give the customer the choice. This also shows them that you have really taken the time to solve their problem/issue, and when you give people options, they feel more empowered. They are in control of their experience again.

Step 5: EXECUTE

- Take action
- Give an accurate time estimate, if required
- Inform your team and manager about what you have done

Once your customer has agreed with the option, then you can go ahead and take action. If there is going to be a time delay in implementing the option, make sure you are truthful about how much time is required.

For example, if you need to change the seat of a passenger during boarding, don't say, "Just give me a couple of minutes," when you know you have to wait for boarding to be over in order to make the seat change. I hate that. I have five kids, and never mind my position in the airline industry, this has happened to me.

For the record, any customer who is also a parent with children in the customer service experience hears, "a couple of minutes," and thinks it means TWO MINUTES. One hundred and twenty seconds. Children are not as patient as adults, and a lot louder when they want to register a complaint.

What I wish the crew would say is, "As soon as all the passengers are on board, I will move you to your new seat, but just to let you know that generally, this can take at least 30 minutes. But I will come back to you." Honesty like that goes a long way with customers awaiting solutions to their experiences.

Have you ever been on a flight and your seat is the only one where the entertainment system isn't working? I hate that too. I'm sitting there with nothing to do while fellow passengers all around me are tuning in to the latest blockbuster hits. Then to make matters worse, when I finally get the attention of one of the crew, they say, "I'll come back to you in a minute."

No. They won't. That's not true. And every minute feels like ten minutes when you're the only person without access to the movies. Grrr.

My husband is always ordering ketchup for his chips in restaurants. It annoys him to no end when he asks for ketchup after the food has arrived and then has to sit there, watching his food get cold while waiting for the ketchup. It's probably only three to five minutes to be fair, but it feels like forever, because I feel like I have to wait too. Both of us, staring hungrily at perfectly good plates of food, refusing to eat until the ketchup arrives. Yes, it is self-imposed torture, but it's torture nonetheless, and the only relief that can come must be delivered by the waiter.

That is how all customers feel when you say, "I'll be back in a couple of minutes," and you're not. If you know it is going to take 30 minutes then tell them, at least give them the courtesy of setting their expectations accurately.

Step 6: REVIEW

- Make sure you go back to the customer
- Ask if everything is okay now
- If required by your company, make sure a report is submitted – or at least notify your line manager

Reports are important because if the customer contacts your company after the experience, your team will have all of the information needed to respond. Recently I received a passenger complaint that detailed the customer had not been served any food at all during a six-hour flight and he was threatening to open a court case against us. The cabin crew had done their job and submitted a detailed report about what had happened, and even took a photo of the meal that had been served to the passenger (anticipating the possible future complaint). Reporting helps your team to protect each other.

I love examples like this because I get to be proud of my team and recognize their efforts. How important do you think it is to recognize your team for not just exceeding expectations but for also doing their job?

Giving praise is one of the most powerful things you can offer as a leader, and it's free. It makes the recipient feel good about themselves, it can help drive motivation to continue the behavior you have given the praise for, and it can help to boost their performance.

When you've empowered your team, and they do well, a compliment extended to them is a compliment extended to you. They did well all on their own, without your interference, and without micromanagement. It's a bit like when my son started to eat all his dinner all on his own. When he could hold the spoon by himself and get more food in his mouth than on the floor, I was proud. I told him so. I told him I was proud of him and that he had done a good job. But secretly, I was proud of myself too. He was eating on his own, he felt empowered, and that meant that I had done a good job too.

Putting it into practice

I'm in the airline industry, so let's take an example from there and see if we can make this process more practical for you. Imagine yourself as a member of the inflight services crew of an IntrepidAir flight. You've almost finished a six-hour flight with tea service, meal service, giving people drinks on demand, sorting out comfort issues, cleaning the toilets, storing all of the equipment, and managing hundreds of passengers with a small instant team of colleagues.

Finally, all of the passengers are in their seats and the captain has turned on the fasten seatbelt sign. The window shades are open, and the tray tables are stowed. You turn to take your seat in the galley, and you notice a passenger has not put a seatbelt on their infant. You politely approach the passenger, and they politely refuse. Fearing an outburst from their child, and fatigued from the flight, the customer begins to argue with you. The customer is clearly in the wrong, but you're a customer service wizard now... so what do you do?

1. Listen:
   - What is the actual problem? A passenger is refusing to fasten the infant seatbelt for their infant.

2. Evaluate Options:
   a. Politely inform the passenger that it is a requirement and for the safety of the child and offer to help her. Use terminology like 'it is only for a couple of minutes, I can help you, I know it is frustrating. I have a child too and so I understand it can be difficult'. If they still do not comply, reinforce it is for the safety of the child and that you will have to inform the flight crew. Finish securing, inform the flight crew and take your seat for landing. Write a report.
   b. Become a 'police officer' insisting that she MUST do it otherwise the aircraft will not land.
   c. Ask another crew member to try and speak to the mother.
   d. Argue with the mother and escalate the situation to the point that you end up having a significant public issue.

3. Costs vs. Benefits of each option:
   a. Medium/high likelihood to solve the problem and low cost (you have informed the passenger it is for the safety, you have informed the captain, you will write a report, the situation has not been escalated) – acceptable.
   b. Low likelihood that it will solve the problem as your approach will most likely escalate the situation, and it's

high cost (passenger will unlikely fly with IntrepidAir again because of your approach, and passengers seated around her will also see the situation and may be unlikely to fly with us again as well) – unacceptable

c. Medium likelihood to solve the problem and low to medium costs (depending on time restraints) – acceptable to acceptable with a cost

d. Not going to solve the problem, and very high costs – unacceptable

4. Make a Decision
   - Option C (if there's time) followed by Option A. It's not ideal to have an unsecured child on the plane during landing but escalating the situation will not likely lead to the desired outcome anyway. I mean, are you really going to wrestle a mom and baby into a seatbelt with minutes left to go and a crowd of customers watching? Yikes!

5. Implement
   - You ask another team member to speak to the passenger. If that fails, then you finish securing the cabin, inform the flight crew, and take your seat for landing.

6. Monitor/Follow-up
   - Make a report about what happened, including a description of the issue, the options you considered, your rationale for choosing the option you chose, and the outcome of the decision.

Being empowered in customer service means that you'll need to make decisions not only to turn around a bad customer experience into a good one, but you'll need to do it in a way that doesn't hurt your economic community. The best way is to start by listening. Then try to put yourself in your customer's shoes and imagine what the experience might be like for them. Try to come up with as many possible solutions as you can and eliminate those that will be too costly for your team. Give the customer a choice between the remaining options, so they feel empowered as well, by helping to solve their own problem. Then make it happen and go back to check and see if the solution they have chosen is enough to satisfy them.

If your customer doesn't want any of the options provided, perhaps you can reconsider offering them the ones you've eliminated. Perhaps a vegetarian passenger without a vegetarian meal would be quite happy with two-minute noodles. Yes, there is a small cost involved, but it's nothing compared to the cost of that customer getting nothing instead of something.

You won't satisfy every customer every time, but you can definitely execute more turnarounds by using a systematic approach than by improvising or imposing something without considering both empathy and options.

As a leader/manager in customer service, your team must be aware of the options available to them for executing turnarounds. And remember, every turnaround is an opportunity both to improve on the service for next time and to recognize the teammate that made the big save on behalf of your team. A good save deserves a round of applause.

9

COACHING

A couple of times of year Dubai has a fog crisis which cripples the city and usually results in all flights from DXB being diverted, delayed, or sometimes canceled. At IntrepidAir we are prepared for days like this. For flights that go out or might return delayed, we load disruption boxes on board. A disruption box contains a number of non-perishable snacks, like maybe a chocolate bar, muffin, a granola bar, crackers, and a small water. Even though we are a low-cost airline and food is provided only for a fee onboard, we make an effort to keep our customers happy and comfortable during disruptions to their flight schedule.

On one of these foggy days, a flight returning to Dubai was delayed at their departure airport waiting for the fog in Dubai to subside. The passengers were delayed for close to four hours waiting to take off. The crew brought out the disruption boxes that had been loaded and found that they were more than 30 boxes short of what they needed to serve all of the passengers on board.

The senior cabin crew member had an idea of what to do but decided not to tell her crew. She had been through my 'Kind of Person' course and immediately recognized this as an opportunity to practice her coaching skills. So instead, she gathered the crew together in the galley, framed the problem for them, and asked them for their ideas. One suggested that they serve the women and children first, and then offer boxes to as many of the men as they could. Another suggested that they ask for volunteers to give up their disruption boxes, hoping that enough people would volunteer to make up the gap.

She remembered from her training that she didn't want to tell her crew her idea, because she knew that would create a bias toward her idea as the default solution, and her crew would not learn to solve the problem themselves. So, she asked open-ended questions, such as:

What if we run out of boxes, what will we do for the passengers that don't get one?

Do the boxes need to remain closed when we serve them?

Can items from one box be removed and placed in another box?

Do all the passengers on board require every item in the box?

Asking questions in this way allowed her crew to solve the problem themselves. And sure enough, it wasn't long before they figured out the optimal solution. They brought out five large serving trays, and one by one emptied all the disruption boxes, sorting each item from them into one of the serving trays. Then they had five baskets of similar items. Starting with the women and children, they offered each passenger three items of their choice. In this way, they had enough supplies to go around, and all the passengers were served something that they had chosen themselves, which helped them feel empowered in the situation. In the end, they had leftovers, so passengers who wanted a little bit more could ask for it.

It was a clever solution. But what made this an amazing experience isn't the effectiveness of the solution, but the process by which it was discovered. The senior cabin crew member on board had the opportunity to tell her crew what to do but instead invited them into a conversation where they themselves discovered what needed to be done. She learned to coach, her crew learned to work through the problem, and even the passengers were given a choice in how they wanted the problem solved.

At IntrepidAir, I contrast Coaching Culture with Telling Culture. A telling culture presumes the leader or manager knows how to reach a solution and knows the answer to the question. A coaching culture assumes that the employee can find the answer on their own.

Coaching is based on the idea that people work out problems for themselves. The act of self-learning is called insight. A new mental map doesn't form in our brain when we're told something. In contrast, when we gain insight through our own exploration of something, we do. To have insight means creating new mental maps, not just being told what to do. It's that simple.

Coaching provides valuable insight (i.e., asking questions) in a much more brain-friendly way than providing answers. In order to take meaningful action, we need to devise a new blueprint for tackling the same problems in the future. Compliance is driven by telling and competence by insight.

Recall a time when you were thinking about a problem, and you had an 'aha' moment – that moment when you formed a new mental map. How did that make you feel? It must have been great! Your brain rewarded you for having that insight by giving you a hit of a neurochemical called dopamine. You loved it, and as a result, your brain registered both the solution to the problem and the process of solving it, as a delightful experience. It became memorable for you.

If you ask the right kinds of questions, your people will have the opportunity for their own insights. They can make the connections themselves and make their own maps for solving the problem. So, coaching that reinforces insight and the opportunity to practice a new skill is a far stronger learning tool than telling someone what to do.

For example, let's say you're the senior cabin crew member on a flight with IntrepidAir, and your new cabin crew member is taking a long time to do their security checks. You know how to do it because you have more experience than they do, so you assume that the best way to help her is to tell her what to do next. You expect things to go smoothly and quickly because you've done so, right? Not likely.

Our assumption in a 'telling culture' is that the other person is missing key information, and all they need is the right bit of data. Once they have that missing information they will be able to get done what needs to get done. You have the info and sharing it with your team is probably the best thing you can do. Right?

There would be thousands of management books available to you telling you how to tell your people what to do if it was only a lack of information preventing them from taking action. However, these books don't exist… because missing information isn't the main issue. Something else is.

I love what Keith Webb outlines as the "4 reasons telling people what to do doesn't work":[13]

1. People interpret your information differently
2. People don't have the skills to put your information into practice
3. People don't believe what you believe
4. People are motivated differently

Let's discuss them.

People interpret your information differently

When I was a Purser at Emirates airline, I had a new crew member working in first class, and she was from Korea. She had not done that galley position before. Now for you to understand, the galley in the first-class cabin on Emirates has a lot of moving parts. The menu is extensive, there are endless types of glassware, plates, cutlery, etc. You need to know the layout, and you need to know what has been used and what hasn't been used. It's like a complex kind of dance involving thousands of potential combinations of customer expectations, available options, available materials and equipment, policies and procedures, and

---

13   https://keithwebb.com/stop-telling-people/

flight regulations. Learning how to navigate this dance takes a good deal of time and experience.

It was the last service before landing in Melbourne (a fourteen-hour flight). I brought some used dishes in from the cabin to the galley, and we were running out of space to put away dirty cutlery and plates. So, I said to her "just stick them in there" and I pointed to a cart I knew had space inside. She looked at me with a blank stare and said, "What does 'stick in there' mean? I can't stick plates anywhere." And she was right. I hadn't meant to literally stick them somewhere, which is what she thought I meant. Sticking plates into carts wasn't a meaningful instruction for her, and it definitely wasn't a helpful direction for her that might lead to an insight or build her own mental map.

A helpful response from me might have been, "Do you have any spare space anywhere for me to put the plates?" That would have invited her to solve the problem, which would have required her to have the insight about the cart with space inside, which would have produced in her mind the mental map she could use to solve a similar problem on all subsequent flights she would ever serve on.

Can you think of a time when you needed a team member's support in customer service but they simply didn't understand the information you gave them?

People don't have the skills to put your information into practice

Back in the day at Emirates airline, we used to set up beautiful desserts, cheese and fruit trolleys in business class. Now, business class is the most demanding cabin to work in at Emirates, operated by a cabin supervisor and three trained business class crew. One day I was both the cabin supervisor and the business class galley operator, and instead of having two more business class crew who were trained, I had two economy trained crew who had been pulled out from standby and were working in business class but had never had any training. You can imagine the challenge of having to manage the whole flight and operate the business class cabin with untrained teammates.

I asked one of the rookies to go to the first-class stowage to get the business class trolleys and bring them back to business class and assemble them. The trolleys were big steel things that folded down. They were heavy and complex, with lots of moving parts. She managed to find where they were, and bring them to me, but couldn't work out how to actually assemble them. Telling her what to do was useless… she'd never been trained how to do it. She didn't have the necessary skills. Was that her fault? No. Was telling her what to do helpful? No.

What I should've said is, "Have you done this before, will you need help?"

Can you think of a time in customer service when you needed a teammate's support and they were willing and understood you, but actually didn't have the required skills?

People don't believe what you believe

If people don't believe what you believe, they are not likely to follow through with what you have said, or they will on that day but will revert to their own way next time. When I was working at Emirates we used to give hot towels to the passengers before every service, even in economy. But the crew rarely did it unless told to. Instead of telling them to do it, I would say something like, "The passengers must be getting hungry, they've been sleeping for a couple of hours. After I have been asleep on a flight I love waking up to the warm, wet towel to refresh."

I often found crew would agree with me and would have that light bulb 'aha!' moment, as they could see the purpose behind the towel and what it provided people as they imagined themselves being in that situation as a passenger. I would say 90% of the time the crew would just start preparing them without having to be told.

Can you think of a time in customer service when you were able to gain a teammate's support – not by giving an instruction – but by helping them to believe what you believe about a customer service activity?

People are motivated differently

"We do what we're motivated to do, not just what we know how to do. A person is usually motivated by what they are passionate about and that which uses their strengths. Take some time to know these things about the other person and look for ways to match their natural motivations to the task at hand."[14]

Patrick is one of my team members that is motivated by seeing his customers have an elevated experience onboard. He buys activity packs for kids that have crayons, activities, and coloring books in them and brings them on board for the kids, entirely at his own cost, just because he likes being able to provide a better experience for his young guests. I didn't train him to do that, and he doesn't get compensated for it by IntrepidAir. He's elevated his own experience of work by elevating the experience of his customers.

Sung is another one of my crew that does this sort of thing. She carries a mini printer on board that connects to her phone. If one of her passengers is celebrating a special event, like a birthday or anniversary, she'll take a photo, print it out onboard, and create a little handmade card for them right there on the flight. She's motivated by the joy she gets from elevating other peoples' experiences onboard her flights. She views her customers as her personal guests and works to make their travel more memorable.

---

14   https://keithwebb.com/stop-telling-people/

If people were like Sung's printer, then we could just tell them what to do, and they'd print out the right picture of what needs to be done. But machines are limited, they only do what they were designed to do. People are much more capable, creative, and intelligent. People don't need engineers to make them work, they need coaches. You don't always have to be a problem solver. You need to work with your team to solve problems and to improve the work of the team. So, let's go through tips on how to use a coaching approach for customer service management:

1. Active listening

Make sure that your attention is focused on the person you're listening to and remember that most of the message is non-verbal. Pay attention to posture, tone, and body language.

- Don't get distracted by what's going on around you.
- Keep your posture open and welcoming.
- Focus on the person you are listening to.
- Make eye contact.
- Resist the urge to prepare a response in your head while you're listening.
- Nod occasionally and give small affirmations like "yes," and "okay," to indicate that you are paying attention.
- Smile.

Be the kind of person who actively listens.

2. Overcome your desire to take over and be directive

This is a hard one, especially if you are one of those people who think they are the only one that can do it best. You know who you are! (I used to be one).

You may not arrive at the same solutions as your team does, or the team may solve a problem differently than you would. However, if you support and motivate them, they're likely to come up with an idea as good as yours or even better. The result will be better if they are invested in a solution they own and own it in the end.

When it's -10C and blowing snow outside in Belgrade, it would be so much easier and faster for me to get my kids out the door by doing up their coats for them. That's especially true of my youngest Levi, who struggled a bit with getting his jacket done up. I was really tempted to keep helping him, long after I knew he should be working it out for himself. Being a good coach at work means being a good coach as a parent too, so for a long time, I simply refused to do it for him. Sometimes we had to wait in the cold while Levi worked out the solution to the zipper and button problem. But you know what, after a few tries, he got it. I've never had to do up his coat since then, and we're a lot faster as a family now that everyone can do up their own coats in the same amount of time.

Be the kind of person who is supportive rather than directive.

3. Always include the 'why' and impact

Always ensure that your team member knows the 'why' behind what they are doing. Add meaning to the task by describing the impact to them, the team, the company, and the customer. If they understand the 'why' and the impact they will more likely repeat that behavior.

Be the kind of person who gives explanations.

4. Model the behavior

Modeling shows that a leader can walk the talk. It's a powerful tool for building credibility. Research shows that people tend to mimic the behaviors of others when they are uncertain about what to do – and they more often mimic others that have status or power.

Be the kind of person who people look up to.

5. Take the time

Don't be in a rush. Take the extra few moments to coach instead of just telling your teammates what to do. The invested time will come back to you in efficiency later when they don't have to ask, and they can solve similar challenges on their own.

Be the kind of person who takes the time.

6. Your delivery

It is your words, your tone, your facial expressions, and your body language that will determine the success of your coaching efforts.

Be the kind of person who is self-aware of their delivery.

7. Watch your words

Your words mean everything – avoid unhelpful phrases and wording – e.g. "Not like that", "I am the manager, do as I say", "Just do what I say". Remember that most people define themselves by the words that others use of them. If you keep telling your team they're a bunch of idiots… they'll almost certainly conform to your description.

Be the kind of person who uses positive phrases.

8. Questions, questions, questions

Use open questions in order to help you (and your team) understand the situation. For example:

- Can you describe the situation in more detail?
- What have you already tried?
- What are some other ways you could approach this?
- If there was another core issue behind this surface problem, what might it be?
- What would you do if…?
- What are the advantages and disadvantages of…?
- Which of all of the possible solutions appeals to you most?
- Which of all of the possible solutions would likely give us the best results?
- What else can you think of that might be relevant?

Be the kind of person who asks questions instead of telling. Be the kind of person who uses open questions to help your team members learn.

Let's look at an example of how these eight coaching tips might work in your context. Imagine yourself in a challenging customer service dilemma relevant to your current role. One of your service team members has approached you to tell you that a customer has a reasonable and shared expectation, and for reasons outside of your control, your team member is unable to deliver what the customer wants. What do you do? How do you coach them through this?

1. Understand the situation – How do you think you can fully understand the situation? Through asking them open questions. Get the facts.

2. Always start by asking the team member – 'What do you think you should do?' Remember you may not be aware of the resources available, and to empower them, you can't just give them the answer – even if you know it.

3. Allow the team member to respond with options.

4. Then guide them into making the decision, without telling them what to do.

5. Use supportive phrases – Words like, "I trust you to take care of the situation, please tell the customer I will come and talk to him once I am done with my work here. Please call me if you need further support, I am here to help you."

6. Follow-up – Once you are done with your work, go and speak to the team member to find out what happened, give them feedback (either "well done you handled that really well" or "okay, so for next time what could you do differently?") And make sure to speak to the customer.

Can you think of a specific time when a team member approached you to solve a customer service challenge? Note it here:

_____

_____

_____

What was your response?

_____

_____

_____

No matter what the situation is, in order to help your teammates reach the insights and build the mental maps they'll need in the future, you'll need to take a coaching approach to respond to them. If you did, and you can see it in your reply above, then well done. If you didn't, that's okay, what can you do differently next time?

Here are some guiding questions you might ask:

1. What do you think you should do?
2. What are the options available to you?
3. Which option would give you the best results?
4. What time limit do you have?
5. How can I support you?

You're well on your way to a more meaningful life in customer service for yourself and for your team. Don't forget by coaching your team and empowering them:

1. Customers get dealt with quicker

2. Having your teammates solve their own problems frees you up to do the things you need to get done
3. It motivates the team when they feel trusted and empowered

You may need to know everything that happens in your service area, but you don't have to personally deal with it. And when things go wrong, of course, you're going to know best how to fix it, and you'll think that the most efficient way to do it is to simply tell your team how to get it done. But you'll be wrong on both accounts.

Telling your team what to do and how to do it limits the range of possible solutions to your own experience, which might be considerable, but it's not going to be as considerable as yours and your teammate's experiences combined. Coaching requires the humility that allows your teammates to discover solutions on their own, and sometimes they'll come up with great ideas that you might have never considered. You might not have the best answer.

Although it takes less time for you to tell them what to do, it certainly isn't more efficient in the long run. Remember my son Levi and his jacket? You've taught them that you have the answer and they should come to you. So, guess what they'll do? Instead of solving the problem, they'll come to you. You might feel important, but you'll guarantee yourself a lot of unnecessary work, and you'll guarantee that your team remains disempowered and unresourceful. Coaching requires the foresight to invest a bit more time today in the learning experience, in order to prevent repeated requests for help in the future.

CONCLUSION

Throughout this book, I've been asking you to try to define what kind of person you are. I'm willing to bet that the foundation of that definition is in the answer to the two guiding questions governing your role in customer service.

First, why are you here and not somewhere else? Well, you're in your current role because it's the inevitable result of all of the decisions you've ever made. You were empowered to not work where you are, you could have chosen to work somewhere else. But you chose your particular role at this time because this is the best way you know of to reach your personal vision for your personal life. That's why you're there and not somewhere else. This is the best way forward for you because if there was a better way forward, you'd be doing that instead.

Second, why are you here and not someone else? Well, you're in your current role because you're a 'good fit'. There are tens of thousands of people out there with a CV just like yours, but none of them were chosen. And you were probably not the only person interviewed for your job. All of the people interviewed are qualified from the standpoint of education and experience, but the others weren't chosen. You were because ultimately your economic community wasn't looking for a 'qualified' person. They were looking for a kind of person, and you're it. You're in your job because of who you are.

So, who are you?

What are the character traits that you have that add value to your experience and education in order to produce the kind of person that would be chosen to work in your current role at this time, and in that particular economic community? This is no accident.

You might consider that the next time you are choosing your service attitude. As customer service professionals, we can get tired, have bad days, and sometimes forget that our customers are expecting us to be at our best each and every day. Don't let yourself slip into a transactional relationship with those who are bringing their money to share with your economic community. You need each other. And for your part, "nothing is too much trouble" should be your attitude toward actively accepting the challenge of encouraging your customer to share their resources with you.

Your service attitude will be an external reflection of your internal mindset. Strive to remain in a green mindset, optimistic, and proud of your work, because it will not only improve the quality of your service to others but the quality of your own experience of that exchange. Your inner voice will be a verbal echo of your mindset, giving you all kinds of recommendations each day for how you should handle the situations you are in. Just remember that the voice isn't you. You can negotiate with it and ignore it completely. It's a recommender and nothing more.

And when you're questioning your inner voice, remind yourself that what it is and what it means are totally different things. What happens is objective, but what it means is entirely up for design. You can choose for your experiences to mean, whatever you want them to mean... or to mean nothing at all. This is a ninja-like skill in customer service. So do your best to keep this in mind when you are choosing your mindset for the day.

Remember that you are not alone. You have a team of people around you that are helping you to win the game each day. Each of your team members brings their own skill and abilities, mindset, and inner voice to the customer service game you are playing each day. As a teammate, or as a team leader, you can do a lot to encourage the development of trust, dependability, structure, and clarity, on your team and to your work. The result will be that you and your team find deeper meaning in the work that you do, and you will experience the impact that each of you is hoping to make each day on the lives of your customers, and on each other as you share your lives.

When things go wrong, and they inevitably will from time to time, you have a blueprint to follow for turning it around. You can listen to your customer and/or team member. Try to empathize by putting yourself in their shoes and imagining the unmet expectation that they are feeling. Identify the options that are available to you in order to solve that problem. Offer a choice of solutions to your customer or teammate. Execute well on their selection. Then check back with them to make sure it was acceptable. Just remember that you are representing an entire economic community, so you need to do what provides the best balance of benefits for both your customer or teammate and the community that is serving them.

You as a leader or manager in the service industry are providing customer services for your employees. You must serve your staff so that they can serve your customers. That's the only way to create consistently effective customer service experiences. If your people are serving both the customer and the manager, then you're very likely to fail. So, stop telling your people what to do, and coach them to solve problems on their own.

Coaching might require you to be more patient in the short term so that your team becomes more autonomous and empowered in the long term. People learn better from working through problems than from being told the answers, so be the kind of person that helps your team to learn effectively rather than dictating their paths forward.

Ultimately, your results are yours, so embrace the accountability that comes with true empowerment. Authority and accountability together is empowerment, and accountability requires feedback and consequences. My hope for you and your team is that living a consistently empowered work-life will mean a steady stream of positive consequences for you all. Better attitudes and stronger empowerment lead to higher performance. Higher performance leads to more opportunities for raises, bonuses, better jobs, bigger teams, and greater overall lifetime earnings. Plus, you'll live a healthier and longer life as a consequence of finding more meaning at work.

It's not a job, it's half of your life.

You don't know how many days you'll get to live, you just know that once each day is over, it's over forever. So, I want you to live as meaningful of a life as you can. If you, like me, find meaning in customer service, then you'll know exactly what I'm talking about. It's time for you to embrace the impact you can make in another person's life today, by elevating their experience into a memory, smoothing a challenge into an opportunity, and embracing your core purpose in life.

Customer service is just a modern spin on an ancient truth. Humans helping each other out is how we have all survived so long and through so much. Customer service is a focussed form of human helping behavior, and you have the privilege of impacting and improving the quality of other peoples' lives today. And if that ancient exchange could be made more meaningful for you, why wouldn't you want that?

So go get it. Build a better experience for yourself, your team, and your customer. What might happen when you discover the meaning already inherent in YOUR customer service?

What kind of person are you?

APPENDIX A –
THE INTREPIDAIR CASE STUDY

The training program that this book is based on has been conducted at IntrepidAir for the last two years, and I'd like to share some results so you can see what we've been able to accomplish with this material. The 'Kind of Person' course has been conducted more than 40 times, and we are still working through our staff list to make sure everyone has the opportunity to spend those two days with me and my team, having the discussions that were outlined in the preceding chapters.

Our Cabin Supervisors have the option to attend, and as of the writing of this book, 158 (72%) have been through the program. The average employee tenure of the attendees is 8.2 years. We've received 140 replies to the voluntary feedback survey, with 96.67% indicating a 90-100% overall workshop approval rating. Here are several typical responses we received:

"It was a great experience with amazing interaction. It was educational and eye-opening for me on a lot of things we do onboard."

"I found the workshop very interesting, meaningful, and brief. It was a good refresher as well as a good reminder of what I am doing and why. I have enjoyed every minute of the program. Thank you!"

"I genuinely enjoyed this workshop. It wasn't boring like some workshops. It was tailored to our role. Specific, helpful and useful. I left feeling that I want to try harder on each flight to be the best cabin supervisor I can possibly be. Also loved Nicole's personal touch sharing her life with us, as it made her more relatable and not just our 'manager'. Thank you."

Our In-Charge Seniors are rostered to attend the program; it is not optional for them. So far we've had 166 attendees with an average tenure of 10.2 years. We received 125 replies to the voluntary feedback form, with an average of 92.5% of attendees scoring between 90-100% for the overall workshop approval rating. Some of the typical responses we received were:

"All I can say is that after this training I feel more empowered to bring our customer satisfaction to the maximum with my team that I fly with on daily basis. I have the right tools, knowledge, and skills to motivate, coach, and make a difference. Thank you for the best two days of knowledge sharing ever."

"I thoroughly enjoyed the training sessions. It feels good to be invested in and have clear guidance and expectations from my management team. This was the first time since I joined IntrepidAir that we had relevant and empowering development training. In the long term, it will serve our cabin crew community very well. I am committed to putting my best foot forward in serving my team and my customers."

"I am very happy to have attended the course, I personally feel more confident to do my job better, knowing that I have support from my management team. It was a great learning experience and I hope to learn much more."

As a part of the training, we conducted a series of subjective self-evaluations for each attendee and employed the Enlightenment and Improvement Scores as developed by Professor Corrie Jonn Block, from Monarch School of Business, Switzerland. By conducting the same survey at three different times during the training, we were able to contrast each participant's subjective view of their overall abilities on the day before the training, taken as separate snapshots both before and after the workshop was conducted, as well as a third snapshot that indicated their view of their abilities as a result of the training.

Their view of their abilities as seen first without, then with the training, reveals a gap in learning where their new paradigms fit. It's a measure of the degree to which their field of view, or known unknowns, has expanded, and so, it is called the Enlightenment Score. The gap between where they saw themselves before the training and where they saw themselves after provides a subjective indication of how they feel they've improved as a result of the program, thus it is called the Improvement Score. Both indices are subjectively measured by the participants themselves, but over dozens (now hundreds) of records, they tell a compelling statistical story.

The Cabin Supervisors exhibited an average Enlightenment Score of 6.95% and an average Improvement Score of 11.95%. This means that their understanding of what is possible based on the 22-question survey has expanded by 6.95%, and in those same arenas, they believe they have improved by 11.95%. Below are the five most interesting results from the Cabin Supervisors:

Questions	Enlightenment (%)	Improvement (%)
I know what is expected of me in my role as Cabin Supervisor	9.9	14.1
I am the best person for my job	7.1	10.2
I understand the need to obtain support and respect from my team members to achieve great results	9.3	12.6

I know how to deal with challenging situations effectively	7.6	15.6
I feel empowered to make decisions at work	10.2	20.9
I feel supported by management in the decisions I make	8.0	19.0

Each participant provides 132 metrics, an Enlightenment and Improvement score, and the indices from all 22 questions at each of the three stages. To interpret these metrics, it's helpful to think of the question as telling a story. Remember that the survey is provided three times. So the first question in the table above might be interpreted like this:

> "I thought I knew what was expected of me in my role as a Cabin Supervisor, but now that I've had this training, I can see that I was off, by about 9.9%. Now that I've done the training, not only do I better know what's expected of me, but I've improved in that knowledge by about 14.1%. I see that there's more ground to cover, but I'm gaining ground at the same time."

Of course, the figures above are the statistical averages of 158 records, so the story that we are hearing as a company is that "*we* thought *we* knew what was expected of *us*, but *we* were off by about 9.9%…"

This also means that their understanding of what is possible in effectively dealing with challenging situations has expanded by 7.6%, but the degree to which they feel they've improved as a direct result of the training in the arena of dealing with those challenging situations has gone up by 15.6%. Moreover, their field of view on what's possible in terms of support from management (my department) has expanded by 8%, but their feeling of being supported has increased by 19% as a result of this training.

The In-Charge Seniors tell similar stories. They exhibited an average Enlightenment Score of 10.69% and an average Improvement Score of 14.44%. Here are a few of their most interesting metrics:

Questions	Enlightenment (%)	Improvement (%)
I understand what contribution I make to IntrepidAir	18.9	21.0
I have a clear understanding of why I am in this company	14.0	14.5
I know what is expected of me in my role as an In-Charge Senior	12.1	13.7
I feel empowered to make decisions at work	12.1	21.9
I feel supported by management in the decisions I make	13.4	21.5

The story our staff is telling us is that their understanding of what is possible in the contributions that they make to IntrepidAir has increased by 18.9%, and their improvement in that (now greater) understanding has improved by 21%. This is a massive indicator of improved employee engagement from our highest customer-facing managers. Likewise, their belief in how empowered they were before the training went up as a result of us sharing with them how empowered they actually were compared to how empowered they felt, so they acknowledged that their definition of being empowered actually increased by 12.1%, in tandem with an improvement in perceived empowerment of 21.9%. Each of these metrics tells a story of enlightenment and improvement.

The results of this program in the organization are remarkable and worth mentioning. Among our collection of metrics for customer satisfaction, we measure customer satisfaction with the cabin crew specifically and found significant improvements in the post-training scores when compared to the pre-training scores. In just three months of starting the program we saw:

1. Customer perception of cabin crew helpfulness and care improved by 20.0%.
2. Customer perception of cabin crew attitude improved by 20.3%.
3. Customer perception of overall cabin crew experience improved by 17.9%.

The Kind of Person program was the only significant change made to cabin crew training during this time, and so these improvements in customer ratings are attributable to the outcome of the program.

I also regularly receive emails from my staff with stories of our people who have been through this program going above and beyond in their customer service activities. I'll share three of them with you. The names have been changed.

Hi Nicole,

I had the pleasure to fly with Amy last week and I was totally amazed by her overall performance. Apart from the feedback form that I have also submitted, I wanted to share her 'make a difference' moment.

In a nutshell: Amy was actively looking for a moment where she could do something extra for someone. She noticed a family traveling with a little girl. Amy decided to approach them and offer the opportunity of a photo-shoot down the aisle of the cabin. She asked for permission to use her phone and snapped a few pics. To my biggest surprise, Amy had her own portable mini printer with her and she prepared a nice takeaway gift for the girl and her family (please see pics below).

Amy also involved another crew member in the setup making it fun for everybody.

Any is a fantastic Cabin Supervisor; her mindset and customer-oriented approach is a great reflection of your mentorship. She will be an amazing In-Charge Senior one day.

Best Regards,
Barry

Dear Nicole,

I would like to express my sincere appreciation to our Cabin Supervisor, Tanya, who went the extra mile and made a memorable flight for a child who was celebrating his birthday.

Due to her friendly approach with our passengers, Tanya discovered during cabin service that the boy was having his birthday. After making sure that all the passengers were served, Tanya approached the In-Charge Senior and expressed her willingness to make a gesture to the boy and his family.

The In-Charge Senior appreciated the decision taken by Tanya and prepared a tray with dessert, chocolates and two orange juices for the boy and his brother. The child was traveling with his parents, a brother and a baby brother.

We were so delighted to see how happy the boy and his family were to receive the attention given by the crew onboard. Please see the attached photo.

Regards,
Henry

Dear Nicole,

Hope you're doing well.

I would like to inform you regarding our In-Charge Senior, John, on the 1st and 2nd October. In my six years of flying, I have not seen such a hard-working cabin crew member as John.

From helping in economy class during boarding to helping with clearance to ensure all trash and meal boxes were cleared in as soon as possible, as well constantly checking on business class passengers, John was trying to see how he could make the flight experiences of his passengers even better. John went the extra mile every time he could. He was constantly cleaning, doing cabin walks, checking on crew, business class and economy class passengers' wellbeing. John gladly served economy class passengers on-demand water bottles and additional tea and coffee. I frequently saw John topping up the tissues and paper towels inside the lavatories and wiping/cleaning the lavatories and galleys.

It was such a pleasant experience flying with an In-Charge Senior that cared so much. The more John worked, the more we wanted to work. He was extremely positive and left us all speechless. John inspired us and was a great example to all of us.

Kind regards,
Jennifer

I wish I could share more of these examples with you, but that would require another whole book. Instead, let me just say that, as a manager, one of the best things about my job is that I get to experience this kind of feedback from my crew on a near-daily basis. I am thrilled to have found a key to making their employee experiences more meaningful in a way that they actively seek out ways to make the flight experience more meaningful for our passengers.

For every email that I receive, I know there are dozens of unsung heroes out there whose good deeds aren't highlighted for me to see but are no less impactful for our customers. I'm deeply proud of my team. They are the kinds of people who I am honoured to lead, blessed to work with, and delighted to fly alongside.

www.ingramcontent.com/pod-product-compliance
Lightning Source LLC
Chambersburg PA
CBHW030515210326
41597CB00013B/913